The Way of Jesus

The Way of Jesus

Edited by

Tony D'Souza

WILLIAM B. EERDMANS PUBLISHING COMPANY

GRAND RAPIDS, MICHIGAN / CAMBRIDGE, U.K.

© 2004 Wm. B. Eerdmans Publishing Co.

All rights reserved

Wm. B. Eerdmans Publishing Co.

255 Jefferson Ave. S.E., Grand Rapids, Michigan 49503 /

P.O. Box 163, Cambridge CB3 9PU U.K.

www.eerdmans.com

Printed in the United States of America

08 07 06 05 04   7 6 5 4 3 2 1

Library of Congress Cataloging-in-Publication Data

[Theologia deutsch. English]

The way of Jesus / edited by Tony D'Souza

p.   cm.

Includes bibliographical references.

ISBN 0-8028-2684-9 (alk. paper)

1. Christian life — Early works to 1800. 2. Mysticism — Germany —

History — Middle Ages, 600-1500.

I. D'Souza, Tony.   II. Title.

BV4834.F6713   2004

48.4 — dc22

2004040373

Contents

vi

Preface

This little book is the most important book I have ever read because it has changed me more than any other. I carried it in my pocket every day for years. I would snatch time to read a chapter at any convenient moment, sometimes while waiting for a meeting, more often while riding in the subway to and from my office. The book slowly absorbed me. Then it began to change me. These changes were subtle at first, and then gradually became more noticeable. I was changing in some indefinable way — changing from within. The book slowly introduced me to a sense of impersonal Being, that is, a sense of reality beyond the merely personal or egoic self. It allowed me, for the first time in my life, to experience freedom from constraints of the personality or the ego and to become aware of impersonal Being, of THAT which underlies all things. I was convinced that if it could do this for me, a modern man living in the modern technological world, it could do the same for others. I therefore decided that I had to produce a modern English translation of the text so that others could share the experience. This is the book that you have before you.

The spiritual hunger of our times has led many people to explore the religions of the East, yet what we learn from them is something that we always had — something we should never have forgotten. I have called this book *The Way of Jesus* because it restores to us the idea that what the essential Christian experience has in common with all the major religions is an ineffable reality beyond cultural or intellectual expression. Like the great enlightenment texts of the East, such as the teachings of the Buddha and the *Bhagavad-Gita,* this book gives the reader an opportunity to transcend ego-centered living and to experience that ineffable reality. In rediscovering this reality, we reach out to all Christian denominations and to all other religions. If we become personally rooted in that experience, we ourselves are personally renewed.

An unknown person wrote this book around the year 1350.[1] It presents the most important philosophical ideas ever given to human understanding and the most pro-

1. The original text, first discovered in 1516 in a monastic library in Germany, was a handwritten manuscript with the title "Eyn geystlich edles Buchleynn" (A Noble and Spiritual Booklet). It was probably written around 1350, and all we know about the author is that he was "a priest and warden in the house of the Teutonic order in Frankfurt." Martin Luther first published the book in 1518, giving it the title "Theologia Germanica." My primary source is the so-called "Wurtzburg" manuscript (1497) edited by Franz Pfeiffer (1851). I have used the Susanna Winkworth translation of this text (1874) to produce this edition.

found spiritual truth. In my view, it is among the greatest mystical texts of the Christian world. It offers us a vision summed up in three statements that have been called the Perennial Philosophy[2] because they appear in every age and in every culture:

1. There is infinite, changeless reality beneath the world of change.
2. This same reality is at the core of every human personality.
3. The purpose of life is to discover this reality experientially; that is, to realize God while here on earth.

In the first chapter, we learn there is a Being that includes everything and that we are part of this Being. The author calls the Being that includes everything "the Perfect," and he calls what is created by it "the Imperfect" as St. Paul does: "When perfection comes, the imperfect disappears" (1 Cor. 13:10) (or in the King James Version, "When that which is perfect is come, then that which is in part shall be done away").

In chapter 1 we learn further that "Perfection" or "the Perfect" "is a Being who knows and includes all things in himself and his own Being. Without this Being, there is no true Being, and all things have their Being in him. He is the true Being of all things and is unchangeable and immoveable in himself, though all things move and change

2. Aldous Huxley, *The Perennial Philosophy*, 1946.

in him." However, "'the Imperfect' is that which has its source in, or comes from, the Perfect — just as light flows from the sun or a candle, giving visible appearance to something. . . . This visible appearance is called a creature, and all of these things are 'the Imperfect' and none of them is 'the Perfect.'"

"The Perfect" is pure Being. This Being underlies all others. It is the substance and the cause of all things. In contrast, created things (which include humans) are "the Imperfect"; they are "in part." Our fall (and all our misery) is caused when we turn away from "the Perfect." In effect, we make a unilateral declaration of independence, and in doing so we claim Being for ourselves, claiming something that is not ours and that we do not have.

Chapter 2 goes on to tell us, "Scripture, Faith, and Truth all say that sin is nothing else but the creature turning away from the unchangeable Good and going to the changeable. That is to say, it turns away from 'the Perfect' to 'the Imperfect,' and most often to itself."

The sun is the only source of daylight. The beam of light that comes from the sun is not the source; it is an emanation and has no light of its own. Our sin and our error lie in our self-centered proclamation of self-determination. This is the sin of pride, and it is the same sin by which Adam and the angels fell. We have separated ourselves and cut ourselves off from the source of the light, the one true Good. "The Perfect" is the Good. We are "the Imperfect" and contain no good in ourselves. We have to find a way back.

In chapter 3 we read, "I myself have fallen a hundred

times more often, and gone astray a hundred times far-ther than Adam. All of humankind could not make amends for his fall, or bring him back from going astray, but how shall my fall be amended? It must be healed in the same way as Adam's fall was healed.

"By whom, and in what way was that healing achieved?

"Understand this: Humanity cannot do it without God, and God might not choose to do it without humans."

This is our way back. We must empty ourselves of ourselves. We cannot do it alone; we need God to do it for us, and our job is to cooperate. God has been waiting for this moment. He shed himself of his divinity so that he could be like us. He wants nothing more than we should shed ourselves of our false divinity so that we may become like him. This is the beginning of humility and the beginning of wisdom. This is the life of Christ beyond expression, which the rest of the book goes on to explain in detail.

Let this mind be in you, which was also in Christ Jesus:

Who, being in the form of God, thought it not robbery to be equal with God:

But made himself of no reputation, and took upon him the form of a servant, and was made in the likeness of men:

And being found in fashion as a man, he humbled himself, and became obedient unto death, even the death of the cross.

Wherefore God also hath highly exalted him, and given him a name which is above every name:

That at the name of Jesus every knee should bow, of things in heaven, and things in earth, and things under the earth;

And that every tongue should confess that Jesus Christ is Lord, to the glory of God the Father.

(Phil. 2:5-11 KJV)

CHAPTER 1

What Is Perfect and What Is Imperfect, and How the Perfect Cannot Come until the Imperfect Is Gone

St. Paul writes, "When perfection comes, the imperfect disappears" (1 Cor. 13:10). You need to understand clearly what is "Perfect" and what is "Imperfect."

"Perfection," or what is "Perfect," is a Being who knows and includes all things in himself and his own Being. Without this Being, there is no true Being, and all things have their Being in him. He is the true Being of all things and is unchangeable and immoveable in himself, though all things move and change in him.

The "Imperfect" is that which has its source in, or comes from, the Perfect—just as light flows from the sun or a candle, giving visible appearance to something, either this or that. This visible appearance is called a creature, and all of these things are the "Imperfect" and none of them is the "Perfect."

By the same reasoning, the "Perfect" is none of the things that are the "Imperfect." The creatures and objects, which are the "Imperfect," can be understood, known, and described, but the "Perfect" cannot be understood, known, or described by any creature as a creature. We cannot give a name to the Perfect because it is not a creature; a creature cannot know, understand, name, or conceive the Perfect because the creature is simply a creature.

"When perfection comes, the imperfect disappears." But when does the Perfect come?

I answer: When it is known, felt, and tasted by the soul, that is, as much as is allowed in this life.

The fault is in us and not in it. The sun lights the whole world and is visible to everyone, but a blind person does not see it. The fault is in the blind person, not in the sun. The sun cannot hide its brightness but must give its light to the world. God also, who is the highest Good, does not hide himself from anybody. He gives himself freely wherever he finds a devout soul that is completely purified from all creatures. We are able to put on the Creator in exactly the same measure with which we put off the creature — neither more nor less. If I want to see anything, my eye must be "single," or purified from all other things. In the same way, where there is heat and light, the cold and dark must disappear. It cannot be any other way.

You might ask, "You say that the Perfect cannot be known or understood by any creature, but the soul is a creature, so how can the Perfect be known by the soul?"

I answer: This is why we say, "by the soul as a creature." It is impossible for the creature because of its creaturely nature and qualities, all that by which it says

"I," "Me," and "Mine." It is this creaturely nature and its qualities, the I, the Self, and the Me, which must be done away with before the creature can know the Perfect. This is what St. Paul meant by: "When perfection comes [that is, when it is known], the imperfect [the creaturely nature and qualities, the I, the Self, the Me] disappears [that is, will be despised and counted for nothing]." As long as we think highly of these things and cling to them with love, deriving joy and pleasure from them, the Perfect will remain unknown to us.

You might also ask, "You say that beside the Perfect there is no Being. Yet you also say that something flows out from the Perfect. Now, whatever it is that flows out from it — isn't that something else — something beside it?"

I answer: This is why we say that beside it, or without it, there is no true Being. That which has flowed out from it is not itself pure Being — it has no Being except in the Perfect. It is like an emanation or a visible appearance, which has no Being in itself. It has Being only in the sense that light from the sun or a candle has being.

CHAPTER 2

*What Sin Is, and How We Must Not Claim Any
Good Thing for Ourselves, because All Good
Belongs to the True Good Alone*

Scripture, Faith, and Truth all say that sin is nothing else
but the creature turning away from the unchangeable
Good and going to the changeable. That is to say, it turns
away from the "Perfect" to the "Imperfect" and most often
to itself.

You must understand that when the creature claims
anything good as if it were its own (such as Being, Life,
Knowledge, Power, and anything else we call good), as if
it were that good, or possessed it, or that it was itself, or
that it proceeded from it — whenever this happens, the
creature goes astray.

Isn't this what the Devil did? What was his going
astray and his fall but this, that he claimed for himself to
be something, that something was his, and that something was due to him? This claiming something and his I,
Me, and Mine, were his going astray and his fall. And it is
the same to this day.

CHAPTER 3

How Humanity's Fall from Grace Must Be Amended as Adam's Fall Was

Didn't Adam do this same thing? They say that Adam was lost, or he fell, because he ate an apple. I say it was because he claimed something for himself and because of his I, Me, and Mine. He could have eaten seven apples, and if he claimed nothing for himself, he would never have fallen. As soon as he called something his own, he fell, and he would have fallen if he had never touched an apple.

I myself have fallen a hundred times more often, and gone astray a hundred times farther than Adam. All of humankind could not make amends for his fall, or bring him back from going astray, but how shall my fall be amended? It must be healed in the same way as Adam's fall was healed.

By whom and in what way was that healing achieved?

Understand this: Humanity cannot do it without God, and God might not choose to do it without humans. It is for this reason that God took bodily form and was made human, and the human was made divine. Adam's healing was brought about in this way, and my fall must be healed in exactly the same way. I cannot do it without God, and God might not choose to do it without me. If it is to be done in me, then God must be made human. I mean by this that God must take to himself all that is in me, within and without, so that there is nothing in me that resists God or hinders his work.

Now God could do this to everyone in the world (that is, be made human in all of them, and all of them be made divine in him), but it would not change me. My fall will never be amended unless it is fulfilled in me personally. Moreover, there is nothing I can do to help in this healing. I can only yield to God so that he can work in me undisturbed, and I can allow him to do his work and his divine will.

It is when I choose not to do this, but count myself to be my own, and say "I," "Me," and "Mine" that God is obstructed. It is then that he cannot do his work in me undisturbed and without hindrance, and because of this, my fall and my going astray remain unhealed. All of this results from claiming something for my own.

CHAPTER 4

A Person Who Claims to Be Good Has Fallen from Grace and Usurped the Honor of God

God says, "I will not give my glory to another"(Isa. 42:8).

This is the same as saying that glory belongs to God alone.

Now, if I claim any good thing as if it were mine, as if I were it, as if I had the power to do or know anything, as if anything belonged to me, or as if anything was from me or was due to me — I would be claiming for myself some honor and glory.

In doing this, I commit two wrongs: First, I fall from grace, as said above. Second, I usurp God's honor by claiming for myself what belongs to him alone, because everything that can be called good belongs only to the True Eternal Goodness, which is God alone. Whoever claims to be good commits a crime against God.

CHAPTER 5

What the Saying "We Should Be without Will,
Wisdom, Love, Desire, Knowledge . . ." Means

Some people say that we should be without will, wisdom, love, desire, knowledge, and so on. Do not take this to mean that there is to be no knowledge in us or that God is not to be loved by us, or desired, praised, and honored. That would be a great loss, and we would be without reason, like animals.

What it means is that our knowledge of God should become so perfect that we see that none of our gifts or will, love or good works come from ourselves but that they all come from God, from whom all good proceeds. As Christ says, "Apart from me you can do nothing" (John 15:5). St. Paul also says, "What do you have that you did not receive? [That is to say — nothing.] And if you did receive it, why do you boast as though you did not?" (1 Cor. 4:7). Or, "Not that we are competent in ourselves to claim anything for ourselves, but our competence comes from God" (2 Cor. 3:5).

When we know these things for ourselves, we and the

creature become less, and we do not call anything our own. The less we take to ourselves, the more perfect it becomes. It is just like this with regard to the will, love, desire, and the like. The less we call these things our own, the more perfect and Godlike they become. Conversely, the more we think of them as our own, the baser, less pure, and more imperfect they become.

It is because of this that we must strip ourselves of them and not claim anything for our own. When we do this, we will have the best and clearest knowledge that a person can have, and the purest love, will, and desire, because then they will be from God alone. It is much better that they should be God's than belong to the creature.

It is a sin and a great mistake if I ascribe anything good to myself, as if I had being or could know or perform any good, or as if anything belonged to me. If I knew the truth, I would also know that I am not that good thing and that it is not mine, nor from me, and that I do not know it and cannot do it, and so on. If I really knew this, I would cease to call anything my own.

However, it is better that God should be loved, praised, and honored even if we vainly imagine that we love or praise God. This is preferable to God being left unloved, unpraised, and unhonored, because when the vain imagination turns into understanding of the truth, then claiming anything for our own will fall away naturally. Then we will say: "Poor fool that I was, I imagined it was me, but all the time it was God!"

9

CHAPTER 6

We Should Love the Best above Everything for No Other Reason Than That It Is the Best

A master called Boethius once said, "It is because of sin that we do not love that which is Best."[1] This is the truth. The best should be the dearest of all things to us. Our love of it should not be affected by gain or loss, honor or dishonor, or anything else. What is the noblest and best of all things should also be the dearest of all things — and for no other reason than it is the noblest and best.

One can order the outward and inward life by this.

The outward life: Among the creatures one is better than another, because the Eternal Good manifests itself and works more in one than in another. Whichever creature in which the Eternal Good most manifests itself, or shines, or works, is the best. Whichever creature in which the Eternal Good is least manifested is the worst among the creatures. Therefore, when we have anything to do with the creatures, the best creatures

1. Boethius, *The Consolation of Philosophy*, Book 3, Part 2.

must always be the dearest to us. We must stick close to them, uniting ourselves to them, above all to those to whom we attribute Godly qualities (qualities that come from him such as wisdom, truth, kindness, peace, love, and justice). In this way, we can order our outward life, and we must avoid and run away from all that is contrary to these virtues.

If our inward life is to make a leap into the Perfect, we must find and taste how the Perfect is beyond comparison. It is better and nobler than everything that is Imperfect. The Eternal is above the temporal or perishable, just as the fountain or source is above all that flows or can ever flow from it. If we tasted the Perfect, everything that is imperfect would become tasteless and be as nothing to us. This is certain, and all this has to happen before we can come to love that which is noblest and best.

CHAPTER 7

A Person Has Two Spiritual Eyes: One Looks into Eternity and the Other Looks into Time, But Only One Can Work at a Time

It has been said that the soul of Christ has two eyes, a right and a left eye. When the soul of Christ was created, the right eye was fixed upon Eternity and the Godhead. It remained in the full intuition and enjoyment of the Divine Essence, and it continued, unmoved and undisturbed by all the incidents, suffering, torment, and pain that occurred to the outward person.

The left eye saw the creature and everything belonging to it. It saw the differences between the creatures, which ones were better or worse, and ordered the outward life of Christ accordingly.

Thus Christ's inner life, seen by the right eye of his soul, was in full possession of his divine nature and in perfect holiness, joy, and eternal peace. Christ's outer life, seen by the left eye of his soul, was with him in suffering, affliction, and grief. This happened in such a way that the inward, right eye remained unmoved and untouched by the suffering, affliction, and grief that occurred in the outward life.

It has been said that Christ experienced in his outer life the scourging at the pillar and the crucifixion. At the same time his inner life, or soul seen by the right eye, was in as full possession of divine joy and holiness as it was after his ascension, or as it is now.

In the same way his outward life, or soul seen by the left eye, was never affected by the inward eye in its work of dealing in the world and the things that belong to it.

The created soul of a human also has two eyes. One has the power of seeing into Eternity, the other of seeing into Time and the creatures, seeing the differences between them as said before, and taking care of the body and governing it for the best. However, these two eyes of the soul of a person cannot both work at the same time. If the soul sees with the right eye into Eternity, the left eye must close and refrain from working and be as if it were dead.

If the left eye is doing its work among outward things, (that is, conversing with the creatures and living in time), then the right eye cannot attend to its contemplation of the divine. Therefore, if you want one, you must let the other go, for "no one can serve two masters" (Matt. 6:24).

CHAPTER 8

A Person's Soul, While It Is Still in the Body,
Can Taste Eternal Blessedness

Some people ask whether it is possible for the soul, while it is still in the body, to look into Eternity and receive a foretaste of eternal life and eternal blessedness. Most people say no, and they are right in one sense. It can never happen as long as the soul is disturbed and distracted by material and outward things like time and the concerns of the body.

If the soul is to taste eternal blessedness, it must be pure, stripped and empty of all images, detached from all creatures — and above all from itself. Many people think that this is impossible, but St. Dionysius[2] says that it is possible, and says so in his Epistle to Timothy:

"To see the hidden things of God, you must forsake everything perceived and understood, everything perceptible and understandable, all that is not and all that is.

2. Dionysius the Areopagite (or Pseudo-Dionysius), 5th or 6th century A.D.

14

Laying aside your understanding, strive as much as you can towards union with him who is beyond all being and knowledge. By this undivided and complete abandonment of yourself and everything else, you will be lifted up to that which is above all."[3]

Now, if this is not possible in our lifetime, why did St. Dionysius teach it and recommend it to us? It is only right for you to know that a master said of this passage of St. Dionysius, that it is possible. Further, he said that it could happen to us so often that we could become accustomed to it and be able to look into Eternity whenever we wanted to. (Learning something new can seem very hard and strange at first, even quite impossible, but if you apply yourself and stick at it, after some time it becomes easy. Like any skill or discipline, what you thought at first was out of reach can be achieved through perseverance.)

A single one of these glances is better and more pleasing to God than all that the creature can perform as a creature. As soon as a person turns inward in spirit, concentrating the whole heart and mind into the mind of God (which is beyond time), all that the person has ever lost is restored in a moment. If one were to do this a thousand times a day, each time a fresh and real union would take place. This sweet and divine work gives us the truest and fullest union that can happen in our lifetime. If you have this, you do not need to ask for anything else, because you have found the Kingdom of Heaven and eternal life on earth.

3. Pseudo-Dionysius, *The Mystical Theology*, Chapter 1.

CHAPTER 9

*It Is Better for a Person to Know What God
Will Do with or through That Individual,
Than to Know All That God Had Ever Done,
or Would Ever Do, through Anybody Else.
Also, Holiness Is in God Alone and Not
in the Creatures or in Any Works*

You must know that all virtue and goodness, even that
Eternal Good which is God himself, can never make a
person good or virtuous so long as it is not in that person's own soul; that is, as long as one is concerned with
outward things through the senses and reason, and one
does not withdraw into the self to learn to understand
one's own life — who and what one is.

The same is also true of sin and evil. All kinds of sin
and wickedness can never make us evil, as long as it remains outside of us. That is, as long as we do not commit
it or consent to it.

It is a good thing to study the lives of the saints, to see
how God has dealt with them, and what he has achieved
in them and through them. It is a thousand times more

profitable, however, to learn who we are, what our life is, what God is, what he is doing in us, and what he wants us to do.

Certainly, to know yourself is an art — it is the highest art. If only you know yourself well, you are better in God's eyes than if you did not know yourself but you understood the course of the planets and stars, all of herbal medicine, the psychology and physiology of people, and had all the skills of everyone on earth. (As the saying goes: "Man, know thyself.") Moreover, the proverb is true: "Going out was never as good, but staying at home was much better."[4]

You should also learn that eternal blessedness lies in one thing alone and in nothing else. If a person or the soul is ever to be made blessed, that one thing alone must be in the soul. Now, what is that one thing? It is Goodness, or what has been made good. It is neither this good nor that, or anything we can name, perceive, or show. It is all good things and above all good things.

Goodness does not need to enter into the soul either, because it is already there, only it is undiscovered. When I say that we should come to it, I mean that we should seek it out, feel it, and taste it.

Since Goodness is One, unity and singleness are better than separation and diversity. Blessedness does not lie in many and "much-ness," but in One and oneness. In a word, blessedness is not in any creature, or work of the

4. Attributed to Meister Eckhart.

creatures; it is in God alone and in his works. For this reason I must wait only for God and his work and renounce all creatures and their works, starting with myself.

It is the same with all the great works and wonders that God has ever done in or through the creatures, or even God himself in all his goodness. If these things exist or are done outside of me, they can never make me holy. That can happen only in as far as they exist and are done, known, tasted, and felt within me.

CHAPTER 10

*Perfect People Desire One Thing: To Be to
the Eternal Goodness What His Hand Is to
People. These People Also Lose the Fear
of Hell and the Hope of Heaven*

Now, understand this: People who are enlightened by the
True Light know that anything they can desire or choose
is as nothing compared to what any of the creatures desires or chooses from the depths of its being. For this reason enlightened people renounce all desire and choice,
surrendering themselves and commending all things to
the Eternal Goodness.

Nevertheless, they still want to get ever nearer to the
Eternal Goodness; that is, they want to have a clearer
knowledge, a warmer love, and a more perfect obedience
and subjection. The enlightened person says: "I want to be
to the Eternal Goodness only what his own hand is to people." The enlightened person always fears not being enlightened enough, and this person longs for the salvation
of all. Such people do not even call this longing theirs or
take it for themselves, because they know very well that

this desire is not from that which is human but from the Eternal Goodness himself. People should not take anything that is good for themselves, as if it were their own, because it belongs to the Eternal Goodness alone.

These people are free because they have lost the fear of punishment or hell and the hope of reward or heaven. They live in pure submission to the Eternal Goodness and in the perfect freedom of love. This consciousness was in Christ to perfection. It is also in his followers, but in some more, in some less.

It is a great sorrow and a shame to think that the Eternal Goodness is always graciously guiding and drawing us, but we do not respond by yielding to it. What could be better and nobler than true poverty of spirit? But when it is offered to us, we do not want it, preferring instead to seek our own selves and our own good. We always like to have our mouths filled with good things so that we can taste pleasure and sweetness. When we have these, we are pleased and we think that everything is fine for us, but we are a very long way from a perfect life.

God withdraws his comfort and sweetness from us when he wants to draw us up to something higher — that is, to a complete renunciation of our own things, spiritual or natural. When God does this, we are in danger then of getting tired and distressed and falling away. We can even forget God, turning from him and thinking we are lost forever.

This is a very grave error and a bad sign. The true lover of God loves him (or the Eternal Goodness) in all circumstances, in having and in not having, in consolation or in desolation, in good or in evil repute. Such people seek only the honor of God and never their own honor, either in spiritual or natural things, and they remain unmoved in all things and under all circumstances because of this. (You can search your own conscience in this and see how you stand toward God, your Creator and Lord.)

CHAPTER 11

*During Life, a Righteous Person Can Be Brought
into Hell and Cannot Be Comforted While There.
This Person Can Also Be Taken Out of Hell
and Carried into Heaven and Cannot Be
Troubled While There*

Christ's soul had to descend into hell before it could ascend into heaven. A person's soul must do the same. You need to understand how this happens.

When you consider yourself without illusion, who and what you are, you will find that you are utterly vile and wicked. You see that you are unworthy of all the comfort and kindness that you have ever received from God or from the creatures. You begin to despise yourself so much that you think that you are unworthy that the earth should bear you. You think that it is reasonable that all the creatures should rise up and avenge their Creator on you, punishing and tormenting you — and that you are unworthy even of that. It seems that you are eternally damned, a footstool to all the devils in hell, and that this too is right and not very much compared to the sins which you have so often committed against God. You do not grieve over your sufferings and you are willing to remain without consolation because they are right and just and according to the will of God. You do not want any consolation or release, either from God or from any other source. The only thing that grieves you is your own guilt and wickedness, because you have offended God, and for that reason you are sorry and troubled in spirit.

This is what is meant by true repentance for sin. Whoever enters into this hell during life will enter into the Kingdom of Heaven afterwards, and once there, will taste that which surpasses all the delight that ever could be had from temporal things.

However, while you are in this hell no one can console you, neither God nor other people. As someone has written, "In hell there is no redemption." Someone said of this condition, "Let me perish, let me die! I live without hope; from within and from without I am condemned, let no one pray that I may be released."[5]

Now God has not forsaken you in this hell. He is laying his hand upon this you so that you will not desire anything but the Eternal Good alone. He is doing it so that you can know that that is so noble and good no one can express its deep bliss, consolation, peace, and rest. In this hell, you learn not to care for or to want anything but the Eternal Good alone. You also learn not to seek yourself or your own things, but only to seek the honor of

5. Meister Eckhart.

23

God. When you know this, you are in the Kingdom of Heaven and can enjoy all manner of bliss, consolation, peace, and rest.

This hell and heaven are two good, safe ways for a person, and the one who truly finds them is happy indeed, because the hell passes away, but the heaven endures forever.

When you are in this hell, you think that nothing can console you, and you cannot believe that you will ever be released or comforted. Conversely, when you are in heaven nothing can trouble you, and you believe that nothing will ever be able to offend or trouble you. However, after this hell, you can be comforted and released, and after this heaven, you can be troubled and left without consolation.

This hell and this heaven come about in a person in such a way that one does not know where they come from and can do nothing about whether they come or go. With regard to these things, one cannot give or take away from oneself. One cannot bring them on or put a stop to them. It is as it is written, "The wind blows wherever it pleases. You hear its sound [that is, you are aware of it], but you cannot tell where it comes from or where it is going" (John 3:8).

When you are in either one of these two states all is well, because you are as safe in hell as in heaven. So long as you are on earth, it is possible to pass often from the one state to the other — even within twenty-four hours, and all of it without your own doing.

But when you are not in either of these two states, you are in the creature and you will waver about hither and thither, not knowing what kind of person you are. For this reason you should never forget either of them, but you should remember them in your heart.

CHAPTER 12

What True Inward Peace Is — the Peace That
Christ Left to His Disciples

Many people say that they have no peace or rest. They say
that they have so many crosses and trials, afflictions and
sorrows that they do not know how they will ever get
through them.

Now, whoever looks honestly into this will see clearly
that true peace and rest do not lie in outward things. If
they did, the Devil himself would have peace when things
go according to his will, but he does not — as the prophet
declares, "'There is no peace,' says my God, 'for the
wicked'" (Isa. 57:21).

We must therefore consider what is the peace that
Christ left to his disciples when he said, "Peace I leave
with you; my peace I give you" (John 14:27). We must understand from these words that Christ did not mean a
bodily and outward peace. His disciples, along with all his
friends and followers, have suffered great affliction, per-
secution, and even martyrdom from the very beginning.

As Christ himself said, "In this world you will have trouble" (John 16:33).

What Christ really meant was that true, inward peace of the heart, which begins on earth and endures forever. That is why he said, "I do not give to you as the world gives" (John 14:27), because the world is false and its gifts deceive us, promising much but delivering little.

There is not one single person on earth who can always have rest and peace without troubles or crosses, and for whom everything goes according to plan. There is always something to be suffered here, whichever way you look at it. No sooner are you finished with one of life's problems than maybe two more come in its place. For this reason, surrender yourself willingly to them, seeking only that true peace of heart that no one can take away from you, the peace of heart that helps you to overcome any of life's problems.

Christ meant the inward peace that overcomes all difficulties and crosses. That peace enables a person to be joyful and patient within, just like the disciples and all the followers of Christ, through all the suffering, misery, humiliation, and whatever else may come.

If you give your whole attention and effort to this, you will certainly come to know that true eternal peace, which is God himself, as far as it is possible for a person to know. What was once bitter to you will become sweet, your heart will remain unmoved in all circumstances and at all times, and when your life is over, you will find everlasting peace.

CHAPTER 13

A Person Can Cast Aside
External Symbols Too Soon

Tauler[6] says, "There are men who take leave of types and symbols too soon, before they have drawn out all the truth and instruction contained in them."

People like this hardly ever understand the truth correctly. Preferring their own reason, they do not take instruction from anyone. They want to fly before they are hatched; indeed, they would like to fly up to heaven in one leap, even though Christ did not do so. (After his resurrection, he remained for forty days with his disciples.)

Now, no one can be made perfect in a day. You must begin by denying yourself, by willingly forsaking all things for the sake of God. You must give up your will and all your natural inclinations. You must separate and cleanse yourself thoroughly from all sins and evil ways.

After this, humbly take up your cross and follow

6. Johannes Tauler (c. 1300–1361), Dominican mendicant preacher, Strasbourg.

Christ. Forsaking your own guidance, receive instruction, counsel, and teaching from devout servants of God. In this way, the work will come to a good end.

Finally, when one has broken free from all temporal things and creatures, that person may become perfect in the contemplative life. Whoever wants one must let the other go. There is no other way.

CHAPTER 14

A Person Is Led Upwards in Three Stages
until True Perfection Is Reached

You can be assured that no one can be enlightened unless that person is first cleansed, purified, and stripped. Also, no one can be united with God unless that person is first enlightened.

These are the three stages: First — the purification, Second — the enlightening, Third — the union.

The purification concerns those people who are beginning or repenting. It is brought about in three ways: contrition and sorrow for sin, full confession, and heartfelt amendment.

The enlightening belongs to those who are growing. It also takes place in three ways: the avoidance of sin, the practice of virtue and good works, and the willing endurance of all kinds of temptation and trials.

The union belongs to those who are perfect. It is also brought about in three ways: purity and singleness of heart, love, and the contemplation of God, the Creator of all.

CHAPTER 15

All Are Dead in Adam and Come Alive Again in Christ. This Is True Obedience after Disobedience

Everything that died in Adam was made alive again in Christ, and everything that was made alive in Adam died in Christ. What does this mean? I answer: It is true obedience and disobedience.

What is true obedience? I answer: It is that a person should be free of the self (that is, of the I, Me, Mine, and Self). In all things you should have no more regard for yourself than as if you did not exist. You should take so little account of yourself that it is as if you really did not exist — as if someone else had done all your works. You should also be completely detached from all the creatures.

What, then, exists? What can we believe to be real?

I answer: Only that which we call God. This is indeed obedience, and will be in Eternity, because there is only one thing there that is desired, thought of, or loved.

Now we can understand what disobedience is. It is this: making something of oneself, thinking that one is, knows, or can do something, seeking one's own benefit in the things around, regarding and loving oneself, and the like.

People are created for true obedience and are bound by right to render it to God; this obedience fell and died in Adam, and rose again and lived in Christ. Indeed, Christ's human nature was utterly bereft of self and detached from all creatures, more so than any other human's ever was. He was nothing else but "a house and habitation of God."

He claimed nothing for his own, neither in his Godly nature nor that which was a living human nature and a habitation of God. His human nature did not even take to itself the Godhead, whose dwelling it was, or anything that this same Godhead willed, did, or left undone in him, or anything of all the things his human nature did or suffered. In Christ's human nature there was no claiming of anything, no seeking or desire, apart from that which was due to the Godhead, and he did not even call this desire his own.

We can say no more about this, or write about it, because it is beyond understanding. It was never described and it never will be, because it can only be described and understood by the One who is and knows its ground; that is, God himself, who can do everything.

CHAPTER 16

What the Old Self Is and What the New Self Is

When you read about "the old self" and "the new self," you need to understand what these terms mean.

The old self is Adam and disobedience. It is the I, the Me, the Mine, and so on.

The new self is Christ and true obedience, that is, the giving up and renouncing of all worldly things and seeking only the honor of God in everything.

When we read about dying, perishing, and so on, it means that the old self should be destroyed, and not seek its own either in spiritual or in natural things. Where this is accomplished in the true divine light the new self is born again. It has also been said that one should die to oneself, that is, to the earthly consolations, the I and the Self, and to all the esteem and pleasure that one clings to, enjoys, and values highly. Whether it is one's own self or any other creature, whatever it is, it must die. This is the true way for the self to be brought correctly to complete renewal.

For this purpose St. Paul exhorts us to "Put off your old

self which is being corrupted by its deceitful desires . . . and put on the new self, created to be like God in true righteousness and holiness" (Eph. 4:22, 24). Whoever lives for the self in the way of the old self is a child of Adam, and despite any efforts for an orderly life, that person is still the child and brother or sister of the Evil Spirit. On the other hand, whoever lives in humble obedience in the new self (which is Christ) is in the same way the brother or sister of Christ and a child of God.

Now, where the old self dies and the new self is born, that is the second birth of which Christ says, "No one can see the kingdom of God unless he is born again" (John 3:3). Similarly, St. Paul says, "As in Adam all die, so in Christ all will be made alive" (1 Cor. 15:22). That means that all who follow Adam in pride, the lust of the flesh, and disobedience are dead in the soul and can be made alive only in Christ. For the same reason, as long as one is an Adam or his child, a person does not have God. Christ says, "He who is not with me is against me" (Matt. 12:30). Now, whoever is against God, is dead before God. It follows, then, that all Adam's children are dead before God. But whoever is with Christ in perfect obedience is with God and alive. As has been said before, sin is in the creature turning away from the Creator, which is in agreement with what has been said just now.

Whoever is in disobedience is in sin, which can be atoned for only by returning to God, and this is brought about by humble obedience. As long as one continues in disobedience, one's sin can never be blotted out. Whatever the person does, it will get that person nowhere. Be assured of this: Disobedience is sin.

However, when one enters into the obedience of faith, everything is atoned for and forgiven, and not otherwise. Even if the Evil Spirit himself came to true obedience, he would become an angel again and all his sin and wickedness would be atoned for and forgiven at once. And if an angel fell into disobedience, he would become an evil spirit immediately, even if he did nothing else.

If one were capable of renouncing self and everything in the world and living wholly and purely in true obedience as Christ did in his human nature, such a person would be completely without sin, one with Christ and the same by grace that Christ was by nature. But it is said that this is impossible, and that "No one is without sin" (see Rom. 3:23 and 1 John 1:8).

Whatever is said, this much is certain: The nearer that we are to perfect obedience, the less we sin. The farther from it we are, the more we sin. In short, whether a person is good, better, or best of all, bad, worse, or worst of all, sinful or saved before God — it all lies in this matter of obedience. Therefore, it has been said: The more of Self and Me, the more of sin and wickedness. So also it has been said: The more the Self, the I, the Me, and the Mine (that is, self-seeking and selfishness) abate in a person, the more does God's I (that is, God himself) increase in that person.

Now, if all of humanity lived in true obedience there would be no grief or sorrow, all people would be at one, and no one would annoy or harm anybody else. Nobody would lead a life or do anything contrary to God's will. What would there be then to cause grief or sorrow? But now, alas, it seems the whole world is in disobedience!

If someone were simply and wholly obedient as Christ was, all disobedience would be a sharp and bitter pain to that person. Even if everyone were against this person, this would not be troubling, because while one is in this obedience this person is one with God, and God himself is one with the person.

Now, all disobedience is contrary to God, and nothing else is. There is no thing contrary to God, neither the creature nor the work of the creature, nor anything that we can name or think is contrary to God or displeasing to him. Only disobedience and the disobedient person are contrary to God. In short, everything that exists is pleasing and good in God's eyes, apart from the disobedient.

But the one who disobeys is so displeasing to God and it grieves him so badly that if it were possible for human nature to die a hundred deaths, God would willingly suffer them all for the sake of one disobedient person, to bring an end to the person's disobedience and that obedience might be born again in the person.

Although no one can be so single and perfect in this obedience as Christ was, it is still possible for anyone to come so near to it as to be rightly called Godlike, and "a partaker of the divine nature." The nearer a person comes to it, the more Godlike and divine one becomes, and the more one hates all disobedience, sin, evil, and unrigh-

teousness, and the worse they grieve a person. Disobedience and sin is the same thing. There is no sin but disobedience, and what is done in disobedience is nothing but
sin. Therefore, all we have to do is to keep ourselves from
disobedience.

CHAPTER 17

We Are Not to Take the Credit for Ourselves When We Do Well; We Are Only to Take the Blame When We Do Badly

Some people think that they are so completely dead to self that they have reached a state where they cannot suffer and are moved by nothing, just as if all people were living in obedience, or as if there were no creatures. They claim always to be in an even frame of mind, so that nothing disturbs them, however things happen — good or bad. Now, this is not true, as we have said. It could be like that if everyone were brought into obedience, but until then, it cannot be.

It might then be asked, Are we not to be separate from all things, and to take to ourselves neither evil nor good? I answer, No one should take goodness to oneself, because that belongs to God and to his goodness only.

Give thanks to the man, and everlasting reward and blessings, who is ready and able to be a house and a temple for the Eternal Goodness and Godhead, in whom God can exert his power, will, and work without hindrance.

However, no one has any right to excuse sin by refusing to own what is evil for oneself, laying the guilt upon others or the Devil and making oneself out to be pure and innocent (as Adam and Eve did while they were in paradise, each laying the guilt upon the other). No one has a right to do this because it is written, "There is no one without sin" (see Rom. 3:23 and 1 John 1:8). I say therefore, reproach, shame, loss, sorrow, and eternal damnation to the person who is ready and willing that the Evil Spirit, falsehood, lies, wickedness, and other evil things should have their will and pleasure, making that person their house and habitation.

CHAPTER 18

The Life of Christ Is the Noblest and Best Life That Ever Has Been or Can Be, and a Careless Life of False Freedom Is the Worst Life That Can Be

You should know and believe, as a fact, that there is no life as noble, good, and pleasing to God as the life of Christ. Yet, to our natural self it is the bitterest life of all.

The natural self, the Me and the I, loves a life of carelessness and freedom. This is the sweetest and pleasantest life to them, but it is not the best, and in some people it becomes the worst.

Though the life of Christ is the bitterest of all, it is to be preferred above all. You will know it by this: There is an inward sight which has the power to know the one True Good, and that it is neither this nor that, but it is what St. Paul wrote about: "When perfection comes, the imperfect disappears" (1 Cor. 13:10). What he is talking about is the Totality that exceeds all the Fragments, and that everything that makes up "the Imperfect" is nothing compared to "the Perfect."

Similarly, all knowledge of the parts is swallowed up when the Whole is known, and where that Good is known it can only be longed for and loved so much that all the love with which one has loved oneself and other things fades away. That inward sight also perceives what is best and noblest in all things, and loves it in the one true Good, and only because of the one true Good.

Where there is this inward sight, a person sees with certainty that the life of Christ is the best life. It is preferred above all and a person willingly accepts and endures it without question or complaint whether it pleases or offends nature or others, whether one likes or dislikes it, finding it sweet or bitter or whatever.

Therefore, wherever this Perfect and True Good is known, the life of Christ must be led until the death of the body. Whoever thinks or says otherwise is a liar. Moreover, in whatever person the life of Christ is absent, the True Good and Eternal Truth will never be known.

CHAPTER 19

We Cannot Come to the True Light and to the Life of Christ by Much Questioning, Reading, Intellectual Skill, or Reason. We Can Come to It Only by Truly Renouncing Ourselves and All Things

Let no one believe that we can have this true light and perfect knowledge, or life of Christ, by a lot of questioning, or by reading and study, or by intellect and learning.

As long as a person takes account of anything that is this or that, whether it is oneself, or any other creature, or if a person does anything, framing a purpose for the sake of one's own desires or opinions, that person cannot come to the life of Christ. Christ said as much when he said, "If anyone would come after me, he must deny himself and take up his cross and follow me" (Matt. 16:24). And "anyone who does not take his cross and follow me is not worthy of me" (Matt 10:38). Also, if he "does not hate his father and mother, his wife and children, and brothers and sisters — yes, even his own life — he cannot be my disciple" (Luke 14:26).

What he meant was this: "The one who does not abandon and part with everything can never know my eternal truth nor attain to my life." Though this has never been said to us plainly, the truth says it — because it is certainly true. For as long as one clings to the elements and fragments of this world (and above all to oneself), if that person communes with them and takes great stock of them, that person is deceived and blinded. Such a person sees what is good no further than that which is personally most convenient and pleasant and furthers his or her own wants. That person holds these, then, to be the highest good and loves them above all else. Thus, such a person will never come to the truth.

CHAPTER 20

The Natural Self Shuns the Life of Christ, Finding It
the Bitterest Life of All; It Always Prefers a False,
Careless Life, Full of Ease and Comfort

The life of Christ is the bitterest to nature, the Self, and
the Me, because in the true life of Christ, the Self, the Me,
and nature must be abandoned, and indeed must die altogether. In each of us, therefore, nature abhors it, thinking
it is evil, unjust, and foolish.

The natural self wants only a life that is comfortable
and pleasant to it. It says (and believes in its blindness)
that such a life is the best possible life.

Now, nothing is so comfortable and pleasant to nature
as a free, careless way of life. Therefore, it clings to that
way of life, taking enjoyment in itself and in its own powers and seeking only its own peace and comfort.

This happens most often where there are high natural
gifts of intellect. This is because intellect soars upwards
in its own light and by its own power, until it thinks that
it is the True Eternal Light. It then proclaims itself to be
that, and in deceiving itself, it deceives others along with
it who know no better and are similarly inclined.

44

A Friend of Christ Willingly Performs the Outward Actions That Must and Ought to Be and Does Not Do Anything Else

Someone might ask, "What is the state of a person who follows the True Light completely?"

I answer, It can never be explained. The person who does not know this inner way cannot understand it. Moreover, the person who knows it cannot explain it. (If you want to know it you must try with all your might to enter into it. You will then find what a person can never describe.)

However, I can say that such a person has complete freedom over outward conduct and conversation — as long as they are consistent with what must be or ought to be; but they cannot be consistent with what this person merely wills or desires.

Often a person will make many "must-be's" and "ought-to-be's," which are false. For example, when a person is moved by pride, desire, or some other evil disposition to do or not to do something, this person often says, "It has to be this way" or "It ought to be this way." Or if this person is driven to anything by the desire to find favor in people's eyes, or by love, friendship, enmity, or the appetites of the body, this person says, "It must be so and ought to be so."

You must understand that all this is utterly false. If we had no "must be's" or "ought-to-be's" but only those that God and the Truth demanded of us, we would certainly have a lot less to do than we do now, for we make for ourselves a lot of troubles and difficulty that we could easily avoid.

CHAPTER 22

The Spirit of God (or the Devil) Can Possess
and Control a Person

It is sometimes reported that the Devil can enter into and
possess a person so that the person does not know what
he or she is doing. This person has no power over the self,
but the Devil has complete control, and does whatever he
likes through this person. (In a sense, we could say that
the whole world is possessed by the Devil. It is certainly
filled with lies, falsehood, and evil — and all of that
comes from the Devil.)

But this idea of possession can work in a different way.
A person can be possessed by the Spirit of God in such a
way that the person does not know what he or she does
or does not do and has no power over the self. The Spirit
of God has complete control over this person, and this
same Spirit works, does, and leaves undone through and
by this person exactly what God wants. This person is
then one of those of whom St. Paul says, "Those who are
led by the Spirit of God are sons of God" (Rom. 8:14).
They "are not under the law, but under grace" (Rom.

6:14). Christ says to them, "For it will not be you speaking, but the Spirit of your Father speaking through you" (Matt. 10:20).

The problem is that for each one who is truly possessed with the Spirit of God there are a hundred thousand, or an innumerable multitude, possessed by the Devil. This is because people are more like the Devil than they are like God. The Self, the I, the Me, and all of that belong to the Devil, and it is for that reason that he is a Devil.

Look, one or two words can sum up all that has been said by all these many words of mine: "Be simply and wholly free of Self." Nevertheless, I hope that by these many words I have explained things in more detail.

Some people will say, "I am completely unprepared for this work, and therefore it cannot be done in me." This is merely an excuse, because they are neither ready nor willing to become ready. They have no one to blame for this but themselves. If a person was striving to prepare, and if that person was dedicated to see how to become prepared, it is certain that God would prepare that person. God gives as much care, dedication, and love to preparing someone as to the pouring in of his Spirit when the person is prepared.

Still, there are things you can do. As the saying goes, "To learn an art which you do not know, four things are necessary." The first and most necessary of all is a great desire, diligence, and constant endeavor to learn the art. Where this is lacking, the art will never be learned. The second is a copy or example from which you may learn. The third is to give dedicated attention to the artisan, to watch how that person works, to be obedient in all things and to trust and follow this example. The fourth is to put your own hand to the task, putting it into practice with application and industry. If one of these four is lacking, the art will never be learned or mastered.

It is the same thing with this preparation. Whoever has the first, that is, a constant persevering desire towards the end, will also seek and find all that furthers it. However, if you do not have that earnestness and desire, you will remain forever unprepared and will never attain the end.

CHAPTER 23

Whoever Wants to Submit to God and Be Obedient to Him Must Be Ready to Bear With All Things. That Person Must Be Obedient to God, the Self, and All Creatures Regardless of What Must Be Suffered or Done

Some people talk about other ways of preparation to this end, saying that we must submit entirely to God, being obedient and resigned. This is true, because all this would be perfected in a person who wants to get to the highest and best that can be reached while in this world.

However, a person willing to submit to God must also be willing to submit to all things, whether they come from God himself, the creatures, or anything whatsoever. If you want to be obedient, resigned, and submissive to God, you must be resigned, obedient, and submissive to all things. You must do this in a spirit of yielding and not of resistance, taking it all in silence and resting on the hidden foundations of your soul.

You must have a secret, inward patience that enables you to take all crosses willingly. Whatever befalls you,

you are neither to call for nor desire any reparation, deliverance, resistance, or revenge, but always in a loving and sincere humility cry from the heart, "Father, forgive them, for they do not know what they are doing!" (Luke 23:34).

This is a good path to what is the best, and a good preparation for the farthest goal that one may reach in this world. This is the lovely life of Christ, because he walked this path most perfectly and completely until the end of his physical life on earth.

Therefore, there is no better way to prepare to gain the joyful life of Jesus Christ than this same way, and to practice it yourself as much as you can.

We have already said something about this, and all that we have said here or elsewhere is only a means to the same end.

What is that end? No one can know or describe it, but if you want to know it, follow my advice and take the right path to it, which is the humble life of Jesus Christ. Do your utmost for that with tireless perseverance. If you do this, you will without doubt come to that end which endures forever. "He who stands firm to the end will be saved" (Matt. 10:22).

CHAPTER 24

Four Things Are Necessary Before a Person
Can Receive Divine Truth and Become
Possessed by the Spirit of God

There are other ways to the life of Christ. In one way, God and a person are so wholly united that it can be said that God and that person are one. It comes about in this way: True, perfect God and true, perfect humanity become one.

A person gives space to God so that God himself is there, but the individual also is there. This unity works continually, doing and leaving undone all actions without any sense of I, Me, or Mine. Christ is there and nowhere else.

Now, seeing that this is true and perfect humanity, there is also perfect feeling of pleasure and pain, liking and disliking, joy and sorrow, and all that can be felt both inwardly and outwardly. And seeing that God is made human here, God is able to feel love and hatred, evil and good and the like, just as a person who is not God feels and takes note of all that gives pleasure and pain and is hurt by whatever is offensive.

It is also like this when God and a person are one, and yet God lives in the person. Everything that is contrary to God and humanity is perceived and felt keenly. Since a person becomes nothing in this union, and God alone is everything, everything which causes hurt to the person is a sorrow to God himself, and this continues to be true of God as long as a bodily life endures.

The one Being in whom God and humanity are united is completely detached from this, as from all things. This detachment is the nature of God, not humanity's or the creature's, because it is the nature of God to be detached, without Self and Me, without equal or peer.

But it is the nature of the creature to seek itself and its own and to be attached to the things of the world, and to seek its own advantage and profit in everything that it does. Now wherever a person forsakes and quits the self, God enters in with his own, that is, with himself.

CHAPTER 25

Two Evil Fruits That Spring Up from the Seed of the Devil, Which Are Like Two Sisters Who Love to Live Together. One Is Spiritual Pride and the Other Is False Freedom

Sometimes it happens that a person works very hard in all the ways that lead to the truth. This person then begins to imagine that the work is completed, that he or she is quite dead to the world, and that the Self is abandoned and completely given up to God. It is at this time that the Devil comes and sows his seed in a person's heart. From this seed two fruits spring up. One is spiritual pride and the other is a false, lawless freedom. These are like two sisters who love to be together.

This is how it starts: The Devil puffs up a person to think he or she is spiritually adept and is so close to God that he or she no longer needs the scriptures, or teaching, but is completely beyond any need at all. Then there arises in this person a false peace and self-satisfaction, and the person thinks, "Now I am above everybody else, because I know and understand more than anybody in the world. It is only reasonable, therefore, that I should be the ruler and master of all created beings. They should all, especially all people, be subject to me and serve my every need."

Then the puffed-up person wants this and seeks it, taking it gladly from everyone, presuming to be well worthy of it all. This person thinks it is nothing less than what is due and considers others no better than dumb animals. This person claims to be worthy of everything which ministers to the body and the natural self. In profit, pleasure, or every pastime and amusement, this person seeks it and takes it whenever the opportunity arises.

Moreover, whatever is done for this person seems all too little because he or she claims to be worthy of much more honor than can ever be paid. If any individuals serve or are subject to this person, they are told they have faithful, noble hearts, and a great love of the poor (even if they are downright thieves and murderers). The proud person praises followers and seeks them out wherever they may be. However, this person does not seek those who do not take orders or are not obedient. No, it is far more likely that this person will blame them and speak ill of them, even if they are as holy as St. Peter himself.

Since this proud and puffed-up spirit thinks that it does not need Scripture or instruction (or anything else for that matter), it ignores the admonitions, laws, and precepts of the Church, including the Sacraments. It mocks all of them and anyone who follows them or holds them to be sacred. Here we may plainly see that these two sisters live together.

Moreover, since this puffed-up pride thinks that it knows and understands more than anybody else, it chooses to talk more than anybody else. It wants only its own opinions and speeches listened to, and it holds everything that others think and say in derision, and as stupidity and error.

CHAPTER 26

True Poverty of Spirit and Humility, and How to Distinguish the Lawful Free People Whom the Truth Has Set Free

Where there is true poverty of spirit and true humility things are not at all as they are described in the previous chapter. This is because a person has to discover for oneself, and to know it with certainty, that, relying on the self and individual power, he or she is nothing, has nothing, and is capable of nothing but weakness and evil.

It follows that this person finds he or she is completely unworthy of all that has been, or ever will be, done for the person by God or by anybody else. Seeing that a debt is owed to God, and by implication, to all created things, the truly humble person then learns to have compassion and wishes for a life of service.

This deep understanding causes a change. The humble person does not stand up for his or her rights in any way but thinks, "It is perfectly reasonable that God and all the creatures should have a right over me and oppose me, and that I should have no right to anything and oppose nothing." Such a person does not ask for anything, either from God or the creatures, beyond the most basic of necessities, and then shamefacedly, as a favor and not as a right.

The humble person does not gratify the body or any natural desires, beyond what is needed to survive, nor allow anyone else to be subservient except when it is absolutely necessary, and then always in fear and trembling, because the truly humble person has no right to anything and feels unworthy of anything.

Similarly, this person's own conversation, ways, and works seem worthless. Such a person seldom speaks, and does not reprove or rebuke anybody unless forced to by love or by faithfulness towards God, then doing it in fear, if at all.

A person who has this poverty of spirit and humility comes to see how all people are out for themselves, and how they are all inclined to sin and evil. The humble person also sees that for this reason law and precepts are necessary so that the blindness of people may be corrected, and that vice and wickedness may be curbed and controlled to what is acceptable. Without laws people would be much more mischievous and ungovernable than dogs or cattle.

Laws are also valuable because few people have come to the knowledge of the truth without beginning with holy practices and ordinances, exercising themselves in them as long as they did not know anything more or better.

Therefore, the person who is poor in spirit and of a humble mind does not despise or make light of law, pre-

cepts, and holy customs, nor of those who observe and believe in them. In loving pity and gentle sorrow this person cries out, "Almighty Father, you are the Eternal Truth,
I lift my grief to you, as it grieves your Spirit too, that because of the blindness, weakness, and sin of people these
laws are necessary, where in fact they are not needed nor
right."

(Those who are perfect are not under law. Order, laws,
precepts, and so on are merely a reproach to people who
understand nothing better and don't know the origin of
all law and order.) The perfect accept the law along with
the ignorant who know nothing better, and practice it
with them, with the intention of keeping them from evil
ways, or if it is possible, brought to something higher.

Understand this — all that we have said of poverty
and humility is true, and our proof of it is in the pure life
of Christ and in his words. He practiced and fulfilled every work of true humility and all the other virtues, as
they shine out in his holy life. He also says expressly,
"Learn from me, for I am gentle and humble in heart, and
you will find rest for your souls" (Matt. 11:29). He did not
despise the law and the commandments, or those people
who are under the law. He said, "Do not think that I have
come to abolish the Law or the Prophets; I have not come
to abolish them but to fulfill them" (Matt. 5:17). He also
said that to keep them is not enough; we must go on to
what is higher and better: "Unless your righteousness
surpasses that of the Pharisees and the teachers of the
law, you will certainly not enter the kingdom of heaven"

(Matt. 5:20). The law forbids only evil works, but Christ condemns evil thoughts as well; the law allows us to take vengeance on our enemies, but Christ commands us to love them. The law does not forbid the good things of this world, but he teaches us to despise them. Moreover, he has set his seal upon all he said, with his own holy life. For he taught nothing that he did not fulfill in action, and he kept the law and was subject to it until the end of his mortal life. Similarly, St. Paul said that Christ was "born under the law, to redeem those under the law" (Gal. 4:4-5). That is, that he might bring them to something higher and nearer to himself, as he said: "The Son of Man did not come to be served, but to serve" (Matt. 20:28).

In a word: In Christ's life and words, we find nothing but true, pure humility and poverty as we have described it. Therefore, where God lives in a person, and the person is a true follower of Christ, it will be and it must be the same. However, where there is pride and a haughty spirit, a light and careless mind, Christ is not there; nor is any true follower of his.

When Christ said, "My soul is overwhelmed with sorrow to the point of death" (Mark 14:34), he meant his bodily death. That is, from the time that he was born of Mary, until his death on the cross, he did not have one joyful day, but only trouble, sorrow, and contradiction. It is only reasonable, then, that his servants should be as their Master.

Christ also said, "Blessed are the poor in spirit [that is, those who are truly humble] for theirs is the kingdom of heaven" (Matt. 5:3). That is exactly how it is where God is made human. In Christ and in all his true followers, there is necessarily a thorough humility and poverty of spirit, a lowly retiring disposition, and a heart laden with sorrow and mourning as long as this mortal life lasts. Anyone who thinks otherwise is deceived, and deceives others as well, as has been said above.

Therefore, nature and Self always avoid this life, and cling to a life of false freedom and ease, as we have said.

Now an Adam, or an Evil Spirit, comes, wishing to justify himself and make excuses, saying, "You are saying that Christ was free of self and the like, yet he spoke often of himself, and glorified himself in this and that."

I answer: When a person in whom the truth works has a will towards anything, that person's will and effort are for no end but only that the truth may be seen and manifested. This will was in Christ, and both words and works were necessary.

Whatever Christ did, he did it because it was the most profitable and best means to that end. He did not attribute it to himself or anything else that happened.

You might now ask, "Then there was a motive (a why and wherefore) in Christ?"

I answer: If you were to ask the sun, "Why do you shine?" he would say, "I must shine, and cannot do otherwise, because it is my property and nature to do so. But this property of mine, and the light that I give — it is not of myself and I do not call it mine."

It is exactly like that with God, Christ, and all who are

Godly and belong to God. There is no willing in them, no working, nor desiring that has any other end apart from goodness as goodness alone, purely for the sake of goodness. They have no other motive (or a why and wherefore) than this.

CHAPTER 27

What Did Christ Mean When He Told Us to Forsake All Things and What Is Union with the Divine Will?

Now, continuing from what has already been said (and confirming what Christ himself also said), we are to resign ourselves and forsake all things. Do not take this is to mean that you must not do anything or initiate any action. (As long as we live, we must always have something to do.)

This command to forsake all things is really about union with God, and this cannot be achieved by our own power. Working or abstaining from work, understanding or knowing cannot make it happen, nor is it in any creature's power.

So, what is this union? It is that we should be purely and simply united to the one Eternal Will of God, or so empty of our own will that the Eternal Will flows into the created will and swamps it, swallowing it up completely so that it is lost. Then the Eternal Will alone is left in us to do or not do whatever it wants.

Now what can help us towards this? Exercises, words, or any creature's work cannot help us. This is the way to renounce and forsake all things: Do not imagine that any words, works, or exercises, or any skill, cunning, or created thing can help. You must leave these things to be what they are and enter into union with God. Outward things must carry on. You must do whatever you need to do; you must sleep and wake, walk and stand still, speak and be silent, and all that kind of thing. These must go on so long as you live.

CHAPTER 28

After Union with the Divine Will, the Inward
Person Remains Unmoving, While the Outward
Person Is Moved Here and There

When union with the Divine Will has truly come about, the inward person remains forever established in this union. God then causes the outer person to go about here and there, doing this and that, involved in whatever is necessary and right. The outward person can then say accurately, "I will neither exist or not exist, know or not know, do or not do, nor concern myself with any of these opposing things. However, I am ready, in obedience, to do whatever I need to do, by outward action or inward disposition, to further all that is ordained to be."

So, you see that the outward person has no motive or purpose other than to play a part in the furtherance of the Eternal Will. It is certainly true that the inward person remains immoveable; it is the outward person that moves. Also, where motivation comes from the inward person to the outward, it is only for such things that must be and are ordained by the Eternal Will. When God himself lives in a person, it is exactly like this — as we plainly see in Christ.

Now, where there is this union, which is both caused by a Divine Light and is sustained in its radiance, there is no spiritual pride or any irreverent spirit. There is always boundless humility and a feeling of unworthiness, an honest blameless life, justice, peace and contentment, and all the other virtues. These must be there. If they are not there, the union has gone wrong, as we have said before.

Just as no created thing or action on our part can bring about or further this union, they cannot prevent or frustrate it either. Only the person him- or herself can do this, with self-will, which is a great shame when it happens. Be assured of this.

CHAPTER 29

It Is Impossible, before Death, Not to Be Affected by Outward Things

There are people who say that a person can, while still in the body, reach a state above all suffering and beyond anything that can affect a person in this world, in all respects as Christ was after his resurrection. They try to prove this by quoting Christ's words: "I will go ahead of you into Galilee; there [you] will see me" (Matt. 26:32 & 28:7-10). They couple this with, "A ghost does not have flesh and bones, as you see I have" (Luke 24:39).

Then they interpret these two sayings like this: "You have seen me and have been my followers while I was alive and in my mortal body. Now you will also see me and follow me, as I go before you into Galilee [that is, into a state in which you cannot be hurt or affected by any outward thing]. You will also enter into this state, and live in it, before the death of your body. You see that I have flesh and bones, yet I cannot suffer. You will be the same. While still in the body and retaining your mortal nature you will cease to feel outward things, and you will not even feel the death of the body."

I answer these assertions by saying that Christ did not mean that a person could get to this state without first going through all that Christ did. Christ had to die first before he could get to this state. Now, if that is true for Christ, how can a human get to it without dying first? If this state was the noblest and best, and if it were possible to attain it while alive, then it would have been attained by Christ, because the life of Christ is the best and loveliest in God's sight that ever was or ever will be.

Therefore, if it was not so for Christ, it will never be so with any human. People can imagine whatever they like, and they can talk about it as much as they want to — it will never make it true.

CHAPTER 30

In What Way Can We Be Beyond All Customs, Laws, and Precepts?

There are people who say that we can get beyond all custom and order, all law, precepts, and morality.[7] They claim that all these count for nothing and can be cast aside. There is some truth in this, and there is a hidden lie.

First understand this: Christ was above the indwelling light. He was God, and therefore above all customs, precepts, ordinances, and so on. The Devil is also above them, but with a difference.

Christ was and is above them in this way: His words, works, actions and refraining from action, speech and si-

7. The author is here referring to the so-called "Brethren of the Free Spirit," a seventeenth-century religious cult. His concern in this and in many of the following chapters is to expose the mistaken foundations of this cult. The cult had taken the spiritual teachings of inner freedom and, failing to understand them, had mistakenly applied them to the self and to the physical world. Thus, Brethren of the Free Spirit considered themselves beyond rules and beyond any moral law—and behaved accordingly. The author is keen to discredit them by explaining the causes of their error, and he does this simply and clearly.

lence, his sufferings, and whatever happened to him did not happen through himself. He did not need them, nor were they of any value to him. It is the same with all virtue, order, laws, and custom. Everything that they encourage is already in Christ to perfection.

In this sense, St. Paul is right when he says, "Those who are led by the Spirit of God are sons of God" (Rom. 8:14) and "are not under law, but under grace" (Rom. 6:14). This means that they do not need people to teach them what is right or wrong, because their Master, the Spirit of God, teaches them what they need to know. Similarly, they do not need people to give them laws or to command them to do right and not to do wrong. The same Master who teaches them what is right and wrong, good or not good, higher and lower, and leads them into all truth — he reigns within them and tells them to stick to what is good and let the rest go, and they listen to him. This is the sense in which they do not need any law to teach or to command them.

There is another sense also in which they do not need any law. That is, to gain any advantage for themselves. Whatever help towards eternal life they might get from the aid, counsel, or works of any creature, they already have within them. In this sense, it is also true that we can rise above all law and above the knowledge and powers of any creature.

CHAPTER 31

We Must Not Cast Aside the Life of Christ;
We Must Practice It Diligently and Walk
in It until the Day That We Die

But that other thing which they talk about — how we
ought to cast aside the life of Christ, and all laws and
commandments, customs, order, and so on, paying no attention to them, but despising them and making light of
them — is totally false and a complete lie.

No doubt they would say, "Now, since neither Christ
nor anybody else can ever gain anything, either by a
Christian life, or by all these observances and laws (nor
can they get anything out of them, seeing that they already possess all that can be had through them), why not
just ignore them completely and forevermore? Why
bother to retain them or practice them?"

You must pay attention to this. It is very important
that you understand this: There are two kinds of Light.
One is True Light and the other is False Light. The True
Light is either the Eternal Light that is God, or it is a cre-

ated Light that issues from him, which is called Grace —
both of these are the True Light.

The False Light is of nature or a natural Light.

Why is the first True, and the second False? That is
easier to know intuitively than to explain or write about,
but I will try: God as God has no attribute such as will,
knowledge, manifestation, or anything that we can name,
describe, or even think about.

However, it is the property of God as God to express
himself, to know and to love himself, and to reveal himself to himself, and to do all this without any creature. All
this is in God as a substance, a potential, but not as an action, so long as there is no creature. Out of this expressing
and revealing of himself to himself arises the distinction
of Persons.

But when God as God is made human, or where God
lives in a Godly person, or a person who is "made a partaker of the divine nature," that person embodies something of God, which belongs to God only and not to the
creature. If the creature did not exist, this would lie dor-
mant in God's own Self as a substance or potential and
would not be manifested or worked out into actions.

Now God wills that this should be exercised and
clothed in a form, for only in this way can it be worked
out and completed. What else is it for? Should it lie dor-
mant forever? What would be the purpose of it then? It
would be just as well if it had never existed, maybe better,
for what is of no use exists in vain, and is abhorred by
God and nature.

God wants to have it worked out and manifested, and this cannot happen without the creature. Now, if there were no created things, this or that, or any manifest reality, where would God be? What would he have to do, and whose God would he be? Here we must turn around and stop, or else we might follow this train of thought until we did not know where we were, or how we should find our way back out again.

CHAPTER 32

God Is True, Simple, and Perfect Good. He Is Also Light, Reason, and All That Is Highest and Best and Ought to Be Loved the Most by Us

I want you to understand that God, as the one True Good, is Goodness as Goodness, and not this or that particular good. You must understand one thing: What exists in space or is present here or there cannot be everywhere or above all things and places. Similarly, what exists in time, today or tomorrow, cannot be always or at all times, and above all time. Also, what exists as some thing, this or that, cannot be all things and above all things.

Now, if God were some thing, this or that, he could not be in everything and above everything as he is, and he could not be True Perfection. Therefore, God is, but he is neither this nor that which the creature, as a creature, can perceive, conceive, or express. It follows, then, that if God, as the one True Good, were this or that good, he would not be all good or the one Perfect Good, which he is.

Now God is also Light and Understanding, which gives light and knowledge. God, as Light and Understanding, must give light and understanding. This giving and understanding of light exists in God as a substance and a potential, but not as a fulfilled work. For it to flow out into works (things done and accomplished in the world), there must be creatures through which it can work.

Wherever this Light and Understanding is at work in a creature, it teaches the creature about itself, that is, how it is good in itself and neither this thing nor that thing. This Light and Understanding teaches people that it is True, Simple, and Perfect Good, which is neither this nor that particular good, but it has knowledge of every kind of good.

Now, having said that this Light teaches the one Good, what does it teach about it? As God is the one Good and Light and Understanding, he is also Will, Love, Justice, Truth, and all virtues. All of these are in God as one substance, and none of them can be put into practice and worked out into action without the creature. Without the creature, they remain in God as a substance or potential, and not as a work.

But where the One, who is all of these things, takes hold of a creature, and makes use of and directs the creature, the creature realizes that he or she is part of the One. Where this happens Will and Love, through the One, flow through the follower. And because the follower is also Light and Understanding, the follower can only will the one Good, which God is.

In a person such as this there can be nothing willed or

loved apart from what is good simply because it is good, and for no other reason than that it is good. It is not because it is this or that, or it pleases or displeases the person, or that it is pleasant or painful, bitter or sweet, or whatever. All this is of no concern because such a person does nothing for that one's own sake or name, for such a person has quit all Self, and Me, and Mine, and We, and Ours, and the like, because these are all gone.

Such a person no longer says, "I love myself, or this or that person or thing."

If you were to ask Love, "What do you love?" Love would answer, "I love Goodness."

"Why?"

"Because it is good, and for the sake of Goodness."

If there were anything better than God, it should be loved more than God; therefore, God does not love himself as himself, but as Goodness. If there were anything better than God, and he knew about it, he would love that and not himself. Thus, the Self and the Me are wholly separate from God, and belong to the individual only in as far as they are necessary for that individual to be a person.

All of this must come about in a Godlike person, or one who "shares in God's divinity," or else that person would not be truly Godlike.

CHAPTER 33

A Person Who Shares in God's Divinity Has
Pure Love, Loves All People, and Does
What Is Best for Them

It follows from what has been said that in a truly Godlike person, love is pure and unadulterated, in so far as that person can only sincerely love all people and things, wish them well, do good to them, and rejoice in their welfare.

Whatever others do to such a person, good or bad, love or hatred, that person could only have love for them. Even if such a person were killed a hundred times over and could come back to life each time, he or she could not help but love the very one who had killed so often. Despite being treated so wickedly and cruelly, the Godlike person could only wish the other well, and do good, and offer the greatest kindness possible, if the other would only receive it.

The proof and witness of this is Christ himself, for when Judas betrayed him he said, "Friend, do what you came for" (Matt. 26:50). It is as if he had said, "You hate me and you are my enemy, yet I love you and I am your friend. You want and rejoice in my affliction, and you do the very worst you can to me. Yet I want and wish nothing for you but good, and I would gladly give it to you and do it for you, if only you would receive it."

It as though God in human nature were saying, "I am pure, simple Goodness, and therefore I cannot will, or desire, or rejoice in, or do, or give anything but goodness. If I am to reward you for evil and wickedness, I must do it with goodness, for I am and have nothing else."

Therefore, God, in a person who shares in his divinity, neither wants nor takes revenge for all the wrong that is or can be done to him. We see this in Christ, when he said, "Father, forgive them, for they do not know what they are doing" (Luke 23:34).

It is also God's nature that he does not force anybody to do (or not to do) anything. He allows everyone to do (or not to do) according to the individual's will, whether it be good or bad, and he resists nobody. This is also to be seen in Christ, who would not resist or defend himself when his enemies laid hands on him. When Peter tried to defend him, he said to him, "Put your sword away! Shall I not drink the cup the Father has given me?" (John 18:11).

By this same reasoning, one who has come to share in the divine nature does not oppress or grieve anyone. That is, it never enters into such a person's mind to cause pain or distress to anybody or anything, either by action or neglect, by speech or by silence.

CHAPTER 34

*One Who Wants What Is the Best Must
Renounce Individual Will. Whoever Helps
Someone to Individual Will Helps That Person
to the Worst Possible Thing*

You might ask, "Since God wills, wants, and does the best for everyone, shouldn't he help everyone, ordering things for each person so that things go according to the person's will and the person's desires are fulfilled? In this way one who wanted to could be Pope, another a Bishop, and so on."

Be clear about this: Whoever helps someone to his or her own will helps that person to the worst possible thing, because the more a person follows self-will, and the more self-will grows, the further that person is from God and the true Good. (Nothing burns in hell but self-will. That is why it has been said, "Put off your own will, and there will be no hell.")

Now God is very willing to help someone to what is the best, and is the best of all things for that person. However, to get this, all self-will must go. God would like to give people his help and advice to get to it, because someone seeking personal good and not seeking what is best will never find it. A person's highest good would be and truly is not to seek the self, or self-interest, or one's own end in any respect, either in things natural or spiritual. A person should seek only the glory of God and his holy will.

God teaches and admonishes us to this, and if we want God to help us to do what is best, and best for ourselves, we must give careful attention to God's teachings, and obey his commandments. Only in this way will we have God's help. Now God teaches and admonishes people to forsake the self and all things and to follow him alone. "For whoever wants to save his life [that is, the self, to guard it and keep it] will lose it" (Mark 8:35; Luke 9:24; see also Matt. 10:39). That is, whoever seeks the self, personal advantage, and self-interest in all things, in so doing loses the soul. "But whoever loses his life for me and for the gospel will save it" (Mark 8:35). That is, whoever renounces self and personal things, giving up individual will and accepting God's will, will save the soul and gain eternal life.

CHAPTER 35

*There Is a Deep and True Humility and
Poverty of Spirit in a Person Who Shares
in the Divinity of God*

In a person who has come to share in the divinity of God, there is a thorough and deep humility, and if it is not there, that person has not come to share in the divinity of God. This is what Christ taught in words and fulfilled in his deeds. This humility comes about because in the True Light one sees (as things really are) that Being, Life, Perceiving, Knowledge, Power, and everything else like that belong to the True Good, and not to the creature. One also sees that the creature of itself is nothing and has nothing, and that when it turns itself aside from the True Good in will or in works, nothing is left to it but pure evil. Therefore, it is true in reality that the creature, as creature, has no good in itself and no right to anything. It has no claim over anyone, either over God or over any of the other creatures, and it ought to give itself up to God and submit to him because that is the right and just thing to do. This is the most important thing a person can ever understand or do.

Now, if we want to be obedient and submit to God, we must also submit to what we receive at the hands of any of his creatures, or our submission is all false. True humility comes from this, as it does from the willing submission to God's will. If this were not true and wholly in accord with God's justice, Christ would not have taught it in words and fulfilled it in his earthly life.

This is a true manifestation of God: It is God's truth and justice that this creature should be subject to God and all creatures, and that nothing and nobody should be subject or obedient to it. God and all the creatures have a right over it, but it has no rights to anything. It is a debtor to all, and nothing is owed to it.

This creature should be ready to bear all things from others, and to do all things for others.

Out of this grows that poverty of spirit of which Christ said, "Blessed are the poor in spirit [that is to say, the truly humble], for theirs is the kingdom of heaven" (Matt. 5:3). Christ taught all this in words and fulfilled it in his life.

CHAPTER 36

Nothing Is Contrary to God Apart from Sin, and What Sin Is

It is sometimes said that something or some act is contrary to God, or that it is hateful to God and grieves his Spirit. You must understand that no creature is contrary to God, or hateful to him, or grieves him as far as it exists, thinks, or has power to act. None of this is contrary to God. The existence of the Devil or of a human is from God and either is altogether good. This is because God is the Being of all that is, and the Life of all that lives, and the Wisdom of all the wise. All things have their being more truly in God than in themselves, and all their powers, knowledge, life, and so on. If this were not so, God would not be all good. Thus, all creatures are good. Now what is good is agreeable to God, and he allows it; therefore, it cannot be contrary to him.

What can there be, then, which is contrary to God and hateful to him?

Only sin. But what is sin? Sin is nothing else than that the creature wills something other than God wills and contrary to him. We can each see this in ourselves, because when someone wills something other than I will, or contrary to what I will, that person is my enemy. However, when someone wills the same as I do, that person is my friend whom I love for it.

It is the same with God: Sin is what is contrary to God and what grieves him. When someone wills, speaks or is silent, does or leaves undone, otherwise than as I will, that person is contrary to me and causes me offense. It is just like this with God. When a person wills otherwise than God, or contrary to God, whatever that person does or does not do, in short everything that comes from such a person is contrary to God and is sin.

Moreover, whichever will wills otherwise than God, is against God's will. As Christ said, "He who is not with me is against me" (Matt. 12:30).

Using this standard, let every individual see personally whether or not he or she is without sin, and whether or not he or she is committing sin, what sin is, how sin should be atoned for, and how it can be healed.

This contradiction of God's will is, and is what we call, disobedience. Therefore, the I, the self, self-will, sin, the old or Adamic person, the turning aside or departing from God, all of these mean one and the same thing.

CHAPTER 37

In God, as God, There Is No Grief, Sorrow, or Displeasure, But It Is Not Like This for One Who Has Come to "Share in the Divinity of God"

In God, as God, there is no grief, sorrow, or displeasure and yet God is grieved because of people's sins. Now since God is free of grief, this can only happen where he is made human, or when he lives in a human who has been made to share in his divinity. It is there that sin is so hateful to God and grieves him so badly that he would willingly suffer agony and death if it would wash away one person's sins.

If God were asked to choose whether he would rather live and sin remain, or die and destroy sin by his death, he would choose death a thousand times over. In the eyes of God, the sin of one person is more hateful and grievous to him than his own agony and death. Now if the sin of one person grieves God so badly, what must the sins of all people do? Consider, by this measurement, how greatly humanity grieves God with all of its sins. Therefore, where God is made human, or where he lives in a truly

Godlike person, only sin is complained of, and nothing else is hateful to him because everything that exists and is done without sin is as God will allow it and is his.

However, the mourning and sorrow of a truly Godlike person because of sin lasts until death, or forever, even if that person should live until the Day of Judgment. This is what caused the hidden anguish of Christ, of which no one can tell or know anything about apart from Christ himself, and that is why it is called a mystery.

This is an attribute of God, which he allows to exist, and is pleased to see in a person. It is indeed God's own attribute; it does not belong to the person, who is unable to make sin so hateful. God loves and esteems this grief for sin more than anything else because it is, of all things, the most bitter and the saddest thing that a person can endure.

That True Light teaches us everything that is written here about this divine attribute, which God wants a person to have so that it may be brought into practice in a living soul. The person in whom this Godlike sorrow works is also taught by the True Light not to claim it personally. It is as if the self in the person did not exist, so the person does not feel that he or she has made grief for sin spring up in his or her own heart. Rather, this feeling has nothing to do with the individual but is put there by God alone.

CHAPTER 38

We Are to Put on the Life of Christ for Love Alone and Not for Any Reward, and We Must Never Neglect or Discard It

Where a person has been made a sharer in the divinity of God, there is the best and noblest life possible; in the eyes of God it is the worthiest life that has ever been or ever can be. This life is rooted in that eternal love that loves Goodness as Goodness purely for the sake of Goodness. This Christ life is loved above all so that it will never be forsaken or discarded. One who has tasted this life can never part from it, even if that person were to live until the Last Day. Even having to die a thousand times and being burdened with all the sufferings of the world, that person would rather undergo all of it than fall away from this excellent life. That person would not even exchange it for the life of an angel.

This answers the question, "If a person gains nothing by putting on Christ's life, and it serves no purpose, what good will it do?" This life is not chosen to serve any purpose or to gain any advantage. It is chosen through love and because God loves it. Whoever claims to have had enough of it and to want to lay it aside has never tasted it or known it. A person who had truly tasted it could never give it up again.

Also, whoever puts on the life of Christ with the intention to win or to deserve anything has taken it up as a hireling and not out of love, and that person does not really have it at all. Whoever does not take it up out of love really has none of it. Christ did not lead the life that he did for the sake of reward but out of love. That person may imagine so but is self-deceived. Love makes life light and takes away all its hardships, so that all things are gladly endured. But whoever has not put it on because of love but has done so for the sake of reward finds life utterly bitter and wearisome and would like to be finished with it. A mere hired hand wishes the working day was over, but the person who truly loves the work is not concerned by its difficulty, or suffering, or the length of time it lasts. For this reason it is written, "To serve God and live for him is easy for the one who does it." This is true for the person who does it for love, but it is hard for the person who does it for hire. It is the same with all virtue and good works, as it is with order, laws, and precepts, but God rejoices more over one person who truly loves than over a thousand hired hands.

CHAPTER 39

God Has Order, Law, and Propriety in the Created World, because He Cannot Have Them without the Created World, and the Four Kinds of People Who Are Concerned with This Order, Law, and Propriety

It is said that God is above order, law, and propriety, and this is true, but he gives order, law, and propriety to all things. This is how to understand it: God wants all these things to exist, but they cannot exist in himself without the created world, for in God, without the creatures, there is neither order nor disorder, law nor lawlessness, and so on. To make these things exist, they must be put into practice, because wherever there is word, change, or action they must either exist according to order, law, and propriety, or according to disorder and chaos. Order and law is always to be preferred to disorder and chaos.

There are four kinds of people concerned with order, laws, and custom:

The first kind keeps them neither for the sake of God nor for personal reward but from constraint alone. These people have as little to do with them as possible and think they are a heavy burden.

The second kind of person obeys for the sake of reward. These people know nothing else, nor anything better, than laws and precepts, and they imagine that by keeping them they can obtain the Kingdom of Heaven and eternal life, and not otherwise. They think that whoever observes the most laws is the holiest, and whoever omits even a tiny detail of any of them is lost. These people are very earnest and diligent in this work, and yet they find it wearisome.

The third kind of person is the wicked and deceitful type, those who delude themselves and declare that they are perfect and have no need of law or ordinances and make fun of them.

The fourth kind of person is enlightened with the True Light. They do not observe laws or precepts for personal reward, because they neither expect nor desire to get anything from them. They do everything from love alone. These people are not as anxious or as eager as the second kind to complete things quickly; they would much rather do things in peace and at leisure. If some trivial matter is neglected, they do not think they are lost because of it. They know very well that order is better than disorder, and for that reason they choose orderly conduct, yet at the same time they know that their salvation does not depend on it. Because of this, they are not as anxious as the others.

These people are judged and accused by both the other

camps. The hired hands say that they neglect their duties and accuse them of being unrighteous. The others (that is, the Free Spirits) hold them in derision, and say that they cling to weak and undignified practices. Nevertheless, these enlightened people keep to the middle path, which is also the best path, for a lover of God is better and dearer to him than a hundred thousand hired hands, and it is the same with all their works.

Finally, you must understand that to receive God's commands, his counsel, and his teaching is the privilege of the inward person who has become united with God. Where this union exists, the outward person is taught and ordered by the inward person, so that no outward commandment or teaching is needed. However, the commandments and laws of society are for the outer person and are necessary for those who know nothing better. Without them, they would have no idea how to behave and would become like dogs or cattle.

CHAPTER 40

More about the False Light

We have already briefly considered the False Light, but you must know in more detail what it is and what its properties are.

The False Light is everything that is contrary to the True Light. It is necessarily true of the True Light that it cannot deceive anybody, neither can it consent that anybody should be deceived, nor can it be deceived. The False Light, however, is both deceived and is itself a delusion, deceiving others along with itself. The True Light is divine, and God deceives nobody, nor wills that anybody should be deceived.

The True Light is God or divine, but the False Light is nature or natural.

God is neither this nor that, neither wills nor desires, nor seeks any particular quality in the person whom he has made a sharer in his divinity, apart from Goodness as Goodness, and that for the sake of Goodness alone. This is the proof of the True Light.

The distinguishing feature of creature and nature is to

be something, this or that, and to desire some particular quality, this or that, and not simply what is good without motive. As God and the True Light are empty of self-will, selfishness, and self-seeking, so do the I, the Me, and the Mine belong to the natural and False Light. The False Light seeks itself and its own ends in all things rather than Goodness for the sake of Goodness. This is its property and the distinguishing feature of nature or the carnal person in each of us.

Understand how the False Light first comes to be deceived: It does not desire or choose Goodness as Goodness, purely for the sake of Goodness alone. It always prefers to choose itself and its own ends, rather than the highest Good. This is a mistake and is its first deception.

Secondly, it deludes itself into being something that it is not, because it imagines itself to be God, even though it is nothing but nature. In addition to this, because it imagines itself to be God, it takes to itself what belongs to God. Now mark this! It does not take to itself what is God's when he is made human (or when he lives in a Godlike person), but it takes God's properties as he is in eternity: God as God, without the creature.

It is quite true that God as God needs nothing, is free, is not attached to any action, is apart by himself, and is above all things. It is also true that God is unchangeable, unmoved by anything, and is without conscience, and whatever he does is well done. But the False Light says, "I will be just like that, because the more like God one is, the better one is, and therefore I will be like God and will be

God, and I will sit and go and stand at his right hand." This is exactly what Lucifer, the Evil Spirit, said when the angels fell.

God in his eternal aspect is without contradiction, suffering, and grief, and nothing can hurt or displease him of all that exists or happens. But this is not the case when he is made human or comes to live in a person.

In short, this False Light deceives all that can be deceived. That is, it deceives all that is natural or creaturely, as it is itself natural. Everything that is not God or from God can be deceived, and since this False Light is natural, it too can be deceived, and it deceives itself and teaches itself more deception. It climbs to such a height in this that it imagines itself to be above nature, and that it is impossible for nature or any creature to get so high. It soon comes to imagine itself as God, and it claims for itself all that belongs to God, especially what is his as he is in Eternity, as God, and not as he is when he lives in a person. The False Light thinks and proclaims itself above all customs, laws, and order, and above the life that Christ led in the body and in his human nature. Similarly, it claims to be detached from any of the creature's works; whether they be good or evil, against God or not, it is all the same to the False Light. It claims to be detached from all things like God in Eternity, and all that belongs to God and not to the creature it claims for itself, vainly imagining that this belongs to it alone. It thinks that it is well worthy of all this, and that it is just and right that all creatures should serve it and worship it. It allows for no contradiction or grief; indeed, nothing is left to it but a mere bodily presence, and this remains until the death of the body and the sufferings that come with that. This False Light also imagines and claims that it has gone beyond Christ's life in the flesh, and that outward things have lost all power to touch it or affect it, as it was with Christ after his resurrection. Many other weird ideas spring up from these initial errors.

Since this False Light is natural, it has the property of nature, which is to desire itself and its own in all things, and what is most expedient, easy, and pleasant to nature and itself. Because it is deceived, it imagines and proclaims that it is the best thing for everyone to desire and to do what is best for themselves, each one pleasing the self and following the individual will. The False Light also refuses to acknowledge any Good but its own (which it vainly believes to be Good). If anyone spoke to it about the one, true, everlasting Good, which is neither this nor that, it would know nothing about it and would think it was rubbish. This is perfectly reasonable, because nature as nature cannot know it, and this False Light is merely nature and therefore it cannot know it.

This False Light also says that it has gone above conscience and the sense of sin, and that whatever it does is right. Indeed, one such false Free Spirit, who believed this error, said that if he killed ten people he would have as little sense of guilt as if he had killed a dog. In short, this False Light runs away from all that is harsh and contrary to nature, because it is nature. Also, it is so utterly deceived as to imagine that it is God, and it would swear by all that is holy that it knows what is best, and that both in belief and practice it has reached the very summit. Because of this, it cannot be converted or guided into the right path, just as it is with the Evil Spirit.

In imagining itself to be God and taking his attributes to itself it is Lucifer — the Evil Spirit. However, because it considers the life of Christ and the other things belonging to the True Light as nothing, it is Antichrist. It teaches contrary to Christ.

As this Light is deceived by its own cunning and discernment, it deceives all that is not God or from God. It deceives all people who are not enlightened by the True Light and its love, because all who are enlightened by the True Light can never be deceived, but whoever does not have it and chooses to walk by the False Light is deceived.

It follows from this that all people who do not have the True Light are bent upon their own selves and think much of themselves. They seek and propose their own benefit in all things and believe the best is whatever is most pleasant and convenient to their own selves. Anybody who says the same thing and teaches them to attain it they will call the best and wisest of teachers, and they will follow this teacher. The False Light itself teaches them this doctrine, and shows them all the means to come by their desires. They do not know the True Light, so they follow the False Light, and they are all deceived together.

It is said that when the Antichrist comes, those who

do not have a seal on their forehead follow him, but those who have the seal do not follow him. This is in agreement with what has been said. It is quite true that it is good for a person to desire and achieve what is good for the individual. However, this cannot happen as long as a person is seeking or desiring personal good in a selfish way. If one is to find and achieve the highest personal good, first that person must lose it in order to find it. As Christ said, "whoever wants to save his life will lose it" (Matt. 16:25). That means a person forsakes and dies to the desires of the flesh and does not obey the individual will or the lusts of the body, but obeys the commands of God and those who are in authority. This person does not seek personal recognition, either in spiritual or natural things, but only the praise and glory of God in all things. Whoever loses his or her life in this way shall find it again in eternal life.

Again, all the goodness, help, comfort, and joy that are in the creature, in heaven or on earth, a true lover of God finds in God himself — and indescribably more, because God the Creator is better, nobler, and more perfect than any of his creatures. However, the False Light is deceived and finds delight in the creature alone, and seeks nothing but itself and its own in all things; therefore, it never comes to the right way.

The False Light also says that we should be without a conscience or a sense of sin, and that it is weakness and folly to have anything to do with them. It proves this by saying that Christ was without a conscience or a sense of sin. We answer this by saying, Satan is also without them and is none the better for that! What is a sense of sin? It is that we understand how humanity has willfully turned away from God (this is what we call sin), and that this is humanity's fault, not God's, for in God there is no sin. Now, is anyone knowingly free from sin apart from Christ alone? Will anybody claim this? Therefore, whoever is without a sense of sin is either Christ or the Evil Spirit.

In short — where there is the True Light there is a true, just life, which is loved and esteemed by God. A person's life is not perfect as Christ's was but is modelled on his, and the Christ life is loved, together with all that agrees with decency, order, and all other virtues. All Self-will, I, Me, and Mine is gone, and nothing is intended or sought but Goodness, for the sake of Goodness, and as Goodness alone.

Where there is the False Light there is a false, licentious freedom, so that people grow regardless and careless of everything. They become heedless of Christ's life and all virtue and desire and intend whatever is convenient and pleasant to nature. This is because the True Light is God's seed, and therefore it bears the fruits of God. The False Light is the seed of the Devil, and where it is sown, the fruits of the Devil spring up — the very Devil himself. You can understand this by studying what has been said.

CHAPTER 41

*One Who Is Illuminated with the Divine Light
and Inflamed with Eternal Love Shares in the
Divinity of God, and Light and Knowledge
Are Nothing without Love*

You may ask, "What is it to become 'a sharer of the divinity of God' or a Godlike person?" I answer: Whoever is illuminated by the Divine Light and inflamed with Eternal Love shares in the divinity of God or is a Godlike person. We have already said something about the nature of this True Light.

You need to know that this Light or knowledge is worth nothing without Love. You can understand this if you consider that someone may know very well what is virtue or wickedness. But this knowledge is of no use if that person does not love virtue and continues to obey vice.

On the other hand, if one loves virtue that person will pursue it and practice it even if given a choice, and that person will do it for no reward but simply from the love of virtue. Also, such a person will dislike wickedness, will not practice it, and will hate it in other people. This person loves virtue, finding virtue to be its own reward, and is content with that and will not take treasure or riches in exchange for it. Someone like this is already virtuous — or is on the way to being virtuous. Whoever is a truly virtuous person would not cease to be so if the whole world were to be gained; that person would much rather die miserably.

It is the same with justice. Many people know what is just, but they do not become just by this knowledge. If they do not love justice, they will act unjustly. A person who loves justice will not do anything unjust. Such a person will feel antipathy and indignation towards injustice wherever it occurs, and that person will do anything so that injustice might be put an end to and people might become just. This person would rather die than do an injustice, and all this for no other purpose than the love of justice. To such a person, virtue is its own reward, and virtue rewards that person with herself. That is how a just person lives, preferring to die a thousand times over than live as an unjust person.

It is the same with truth. One may know what is true or false, but without loving the truth, that person is not truthful. If such a person loves it, it is with truth as it is with justice. Isaiah says of justice, "Woe to those who call evil good, and good evil, who put darkness for light and light for darkness, who put bitter for sweet and sweet for bitter" (Isa. 5:20).

Now we can understand how knowledge and light are

nothing without Love. Look at the Evil Spirit. He knows what is good and evil, right and wrong, and so on, but because he has no love for the good that he sees, he does not become good. It is the same if he has any love for the truth or any of the other virtues that he sees. It is true that Love must be guided and instructed by knowledge, but if knowledge is not followed by Love, it comes to nothing.

The same principle applies with God and spiritual things. Let us say that a person knows much about God and spiritual things, even to the point of imagining he or she knows what God is. Without Love, this person will never be Godlike, or share in the divinity of God. But if, along with knowledge, this person has a true Love of God, he or she cannot help but cling to God, and forsake all that is not God or of him, and fight against it, and find it an affliction and a sorrow. This Love makes a person one with God, in order never to be separated from him.

CHAPTER 42

A Question: Can We Know God and Not Love Him? Also, Two Kinds of Light and Love — A True and a False

Here is an honest question: You have just said, "Whoever knows God, but does not love him, will not be saved by this knowledge." This suggests that we can know God and not love him. Before this you said, "Where God is known, he is also loved, and whoever knows God must love him." These two statements seem to disagree. How can you explain them?

We must start at the beginning. The whole question turns on the idea of the two Lights — a True and a False. There are also two kinds of Love, True and False. Each kind of Love is instructed by its own kind of Light or Reason, thus the True Light makes True Love, and the False Light makes False Love.

This happens because whatever Light or Reason believes is the best it portrays to Love as the best, and Love is then asked to love it. Love obeys the command of the Light or Reason and does exactly that.

Now, as we have said earlier, the False Light is natural, and is indeed nature itself. Everything belonging to it belongs to nature, such as the I, the Me, the Mine, the Self, and so on. For this reason it must necessarily be deceived in itself and be false, because no I, Me, or Mine ever came to the True Light or Knowledge without being deceived, apart from once only — in God made human. If we are to come to the knowledge of the Truth, all these must go and be done away with.

A particular trait of the natural Light is that it wants to learn or to know a great deal (as if that was possible). It derives great pleasure and delight from glorying in its knowledge and intelligence, and because of this, it always wants to know more. Never satisfied, the more it learns and knows, the more it delights and glories in it. When it comes to the point where it thinks it knows all things and is above all things, it is at the highest pinnacle of delight and glory. It then believes knowledge to be the best of all things, and from this it teaches Love to love knowledge and intelligence as the best of all things. Knowledge and intelligence then come to be loved more than the subject of understanding, because the false natural Light loves its knowledge and powers (which are itself) more than that which is known. This false natural Light could understand the simple Truth, as it is in God and in truth, if it were possible for it to depart from itself and its own things. (With reference to our original question: This is the sense in which there is knowledge without the love of that which is or can be known.)

This False Light rises and climbs so high that it vainly thinks that it knows God and the pure, simple Truth, but it only really knows itself. It is true that God alone can know God. This Light then vainly imagines that it understands God, and it imagines itself to be God. It says it is God, and it wishes to be thought of as God. It thinks it is above all things, is worthy of all things, has a right to all things, and has gone beyond all things such as commandments, laws, virtue, and even beyond Christ and a Christian life. It counts all these for nothing, because it does not set itself up to be Christ, but the Eternal God — God as God. It does this because the Christ life is contrary to nature, and therefore nature wants nothing to do with it. However, to be God in Eternity, as God and not human, or to be Christ as he was after his resurrection, is easy and pleasant to nature, so it believes it to be the best. (With reference to our original question: This is the false, deluded Love where something may be known without being loved, for the seeing and knowing is more loved than that which is known.)

There is also a kind of learning that is called knowledge. That is, through reading or great acquaintance with Scripture, some people fancy that they know a lot and they call it knowledge, saying, "I know this or that." If you ask them, "How do you know it?" they answer, "I have read it in the Scriptures." They call this understanding and knowing, but this is not knowledge. It is only belief, and many things are known and seen only with this sort of knowing.

Another kind of Love is especially false. This is when something is loved for the sake of a reward, for instance, when righteousness is not loved for itself but is loved for what can be had from it.

Similarly, someone may love others not for themselves but for what can be gotten from them, or they love God with the aim of gaining something by it. All this is false Love and it belongs to nature, for nature as nature can feel and know no other love than this self-interested love. If you look closely at it, nature as nature loves nothing apart from itself. (With reference to our original question: This is the way in which something may be seen to be good and not loved.)

True Love is instructed and guided by the True Light and Reason, and this True, Eternal, and Divine Light teaches Love to love nothing but the one True and Perfect Good. It instructs it to love it for its own sake and not for the sake of a reward, or in the hope of obtaining anything, and to love it simply for the Love of Goodness, because it is good and has a right to be loved.

The True Love loves all that is seen by the help of the True Light. Only the True Light can perceive the Perfect Good, which we call God; therefore, he must be loved wherever he is seen or made known.

CHAPTER 43

What Are the Qualities of One Who Is "Made to Share in the Divinity of God" and What the Qualities of a False Light and a False Free Thinker Are

You need to understand that when the True Love and True Light are in a person, the Perfect Good is known and loved for itself as itself. There is no self involved, so it does not love itself from itself or as itself. It is rather that the one True Perfect Good can love nothing else, as far as it is in itself, apart from the one True Goodness. Now, if it is itself, it must love itself, not as itself or as an emanation from itself, but in this way: The one True Good loves the one Perfect Goodness, and the one Perfect Goodness is loved by the one True and Perfect Good. In this sense, the saying that "God does not love himself as himself" is true. If there were anything better than God, God would love that, and not himself.

So, in this True Light and True Love there is not any I, Me, Mine, You, Yours, and so on. The Light sees and knows that a Good exists that is all Good, and above all Good. It sees also that all good things are part of the one Good, and that without that One, there cannot be a single good thing. Therefore, where this Light is in a person, the objective and purpose is not this or that, Me or You, and so on, but only the One. The One who is neither I nor You, this or that, but is above all I and You, this and that, and all Goodness is loved by such a person as one Good. This saying is also true, "All in One as One, and One in All as All." The One and all Good is loved through the One in One, and for the sake of the One, because of the love that we have for the One.

When a person comes to share in the divinity of God, all thought of self, self-seeking, and self-will are completely lost and surrendered to God, all except what is necessary to function as a person. Whatever happens to a person like this, and whatever this person does or suffers, all occurs in this Light and this Love, from it, through it, and to it again. In this person's heart there is contentment and peace and no desire to know anything more or less, to have, to live, to die, to be or not to be, or anything of the kind, because all these are the same. The only thing this person complains about is sin.

We have already said what sin is: It is to want or to will anything contrary to the one Perfect Good and the one Eternal Will. It is to will or to wish to have a will of one's own. Whatever sins there are, such as lies, fraud, injustice, treachery, in short, all evil, comes from this: That people have another will apart from God and the True Good. If there were no will but the one Will, no sin could ever be committed.

It is as well that we say that all self-will is sin, and that there is no sin apart from what comes from it. This is the only thing that a truly Godlike person complains about, but it is such a painful matter that this person would rather die a hundred times in agony than endure it. This grief remains with such a person until death, and if it is not there, you can be sure that this person has not come to share in the divinity of God nor is this person truly Godlike.

Now, as we have said earlier, in this Light and Love, all Good is loved in One and as One, and the One in all things. In all things, it is loved as the One and as All. For this reason, all good things must be loved, such as virtue, order, seemliness, justice, and truth. Everything that belongs to God is the True Good and is his own, is loved and praised. Everything without this Good, or that is contrary to it, is a sorrow and a pain, and is hated as sin, because it is sin. Whoever lives in the True Light and the True Love has the best, noblest, and worthiest life that ever was or will be, and therefore only it can be loved and praised above any other life. This life was and is in Christ to perfection, or else he would not be the Christ.

Because of the love with which one loves this noble life, a person can willingly endure whatever must be done or suffered, however hard it may be to the natural self. As Christ said, "My yoke is easy and my burden is light" (Matt. 11:30). This is about the love that loves this admirable life. We can see this in the Apostles and Martyrs. They suffered willingly all that was done to them, and they never asked God that their suffering might be made shorter, or lighter, or fewer. They only asked that they might remain steadfast and endure to the end.

The truth about the fruit of divine Love in a truly God-like person is simple, plain, and straightforward, so much so that one could not even explain it in writing or speech — but can only say that it is. If a person has it he or she may not even know it — how then could that person understand or explain it?

On the other hand, the natural person is subtle and cunning, extremely complex, seeking and inventing endless turnings, windings, and falsehoods for personal purposes. The natural person does this continually, in ways that cannot be described in speech or in writing. In this way, all falsehood is itself deceived, and all deception starts with self-deception.

This is the False Light and Life. Whoever deceives is also deceived, as we have said before. Everything that belongs to the Evil Spirit is in this False Light and Life, and it is impossible to tell them apart because the False Light is the Evil Spirit, and the Evil Spirit is this False Light.

This is how we know this to be true: The Evil Spirit thinks that he is God and he wants to be God (or to be thought of as God). In all of this, he is so completely deceived that he himself does not think he is deceived. This is exactly how it is with this False Light and the Love and Life that come from it. The Devil would like to deceive all people, and draw them to himself and his works, and make them like himself. He uses many cunning strategies for this purpose, and it is like this with this False Light. Nobody can turn the Evil Spirit from his own way, and nobody can turn this self-deceived and deceitful Light from its errors. This is because both these two, the Devil and nature, vainly believe that they are not deceived and that everything is going well for them, which is the very worst delusion of all.

The Devil and nature are the same. Where nature is conquered, the Devil is conquered. On the other hand, where nature is not conquered, the Devil is not conquered. Whether it concerns the outward life in the world or the inward life of the spirit, this False Light continues in its delusion and falsehood. In this, it deceives itself and whoever else it can.

Beyond these words, you can understand more than has been expressly written down: Whenever we refer to Adam or the Adamic person, disobedience, the old person, self-seeking, self-will, and self-serving, or to the I, Me, Mine, nature, natural self, falsehood, the Devil, and sin — all of these are one and the same thing, and they are all contrary to God, and are outside of God.

CHAPTER 44

The Only Thing Contrary to God Is Self-Will.
If We Seek Our Own Good for Ourselves
We Can Never Find It, and of Ourselves,
We Neither Know Anything nor Can
We Perform Any Good Act

You may ask: "Is there anything that is contrary to God and the True Good?"

I reply: No, there is not. Nothing is without God except to will otherwise than what is willed by the Eternal Will — that is, what is contrary to the Eternal Will.

It is the Eternal Will that nothing should be willed or loved but the Eternal Goodness. Where this is not true, then it is contrary to God. In this sense it is true that whoever is without God is contrary to God, but in a deeper sense, there is no Being contrary to God or the True Good, because he is the ground of all.

You can understand it as though God says, "Someone's will is contrary to mine when they will without me, or if they do not will what I will, or if they will otherwise than as I will. My will is that no one should will without me, or will what I do not will, or will otherwise than I will. Just as without me, there is neither substance nor life, this or that, so also there should be no will apart from me and without my will."

Just as all beings are one because they are one substance in the Perfect Being, and all good is one in the One Being, and nothing can exist without that One, so it is that all wills should be one in the one Perfect Will, and there should be no will apart from that One. Whatever does not conform to the one Perfect Will is wrong, contrary to God and his will, and therefore it is sin. Therefore, all will apart from God's will (meaning all self-will) is sin, and so is everything that is done from self-will.

As long as a person follows self-will and runs after a personal concept of the highest Good, as if it was for one's own sake and it came from that person, that person will never find it. As long as a person continues in this, one is nowhere near one's own highest Good, and how then can one ever find it?

As long as one does this, that person is seeking the self. Such a person can pretend to be the highest Good, but that person is not the highest Good but only a creature. A person is not seeking the highest Good as long as he or she is seeking the self.

However, if you seek, love, and pursue Goodness as Goodness, for the sake of Goodness, and make that your goal, for no reason but the love of Goodness and not for love of the I, the Me, the Mine, and Self, then you will find the highest Good, because that is the right way to look for it. Anyone who looks for it in any other way is mistaken, because this is the way that the True and Perfect Goodness seeks and finds itself.

It is a great mistake when a person tries to know or do anything from one's own self. It is a terrible mistake when a person thinks that, all alone, he or she can do something good that can earn merit in God's eyes. If this person understood the truth, he or she would see that this is a great insult to God. But the True and Perfect Goodness has compassion on the person who does not know any better and gives this person as much of the good things of God as this person is able to receive. However, as we have said before, such a person cannot find and receive the True Good without changing. This is because a person will never find or receive it unless Self and Me are gone.

CHAPTER 45

Christ Lives Where the Christ Life Is.
The Christ Life Is the Best Life That
Has Ever Been or Ever Can Be

Whoever knows and inwardly senses the Christ life, knows Christ himself. Conversely, whoever does not know and inwardly sense the Christ life, does not know Christ himself.

Whoever inwardly knows the Christ life knows Christ's life is the best and noblest life that can be. If they do not know this, they do not know Christ himself. Therefore, as far as a person's life conforms to the Christ life, Christ himself lives in that person, and a person who does not have one, does not have the other. For where there is the life of Christ, there is Christ himself. If his life is not there, Christ is not there.

If someone has Christ's life, that person can say with St. Paul, "I no longer live, but Christ lives in me" (Gal. 2:20). This is the noblest and best life, for in the person who has it, God himself lives with all Goodness. How could there be a better life than that?

When we speak of obedience, the new person, the True Light, the True Love, or the Christ life, it is all the same thing. Where there is one of these, they are all there. Where one is missing, none of them is there, because they are all one in truth and substance.

Cling with all your might to whatever brings about the new birth and makes you alive in Christ, stick to that and nothing else, and renounce and run from everything that obstructs it. If you receive this life in the Holy Sacrament, then you have really received the true Christ life. The more you receive through the Sacrament, the more of the Christ life you will receive; the less you receive, the less of that life you will receive.

CHAPTER 46

Peace and Contentment Can Be Found Only in God and Not in Any Creature. Whoever Wants to Be Obedient to God Must Also Be Obedient to All the Creatures with a Long-Suffering and Compliant Attitude, and Whoever Wants to Love God Must Love All Things in the One

It has been said: Whoever finds all satisfaction in God has everything. This is true. It is also true that whoever finds satisfaction in any particular thing, either this or that, cannot find it in God. If you find peace in God, you can never be content with particular things, this or that, because God is All. He is One and must be One; he is All and must be All.

Whatever exists as a particular thing is not the One and is not God. Whatever exists and is not All and above All is not God, because God is One and above One, and All and above All. One who finds complete satisfaction in God receives all satisfaction from One source, from One only, as One. It is impossible for a person to find all satisfaction in God unless all things are as One and that person sees the One in All and the All in One, and any single thing and nothing are the same. Where it is like this there is true satisfaction in God, and not otherwise.

Therefore, if you want to be obedient to God you must resign yourself to all things, and be willing to suffer them without resisting, defending yourself, or calling for help. If you do not resign or submit yourself to all things in One as One, you are not resigned or submitted to God.

The life of Christ is a good example. If you want to lie still under God's hand, you must lie still under all things in One as One, and not resist any suffering. That is what Christ did. If you fight against affliction and refuse to endure it, you are fighting against God. That is to say, we must not resist any creature or thing by violent means, either in will or in action. However, we are allowed to prevent or avoid affliction, for escaping from it is not a sin.

Someone who loves God loves all things in One as All, the One and the All, and One in the All as All in the One. If you love some particular thing, this or that, neither in the One nor for the sake of the One, you do not love God. You love something that is not God and therefore you love it more than God. Whoever loves something more than God, or along with God, does not love God, for God must be and will be loved alone, and nothing ought to be loved but God alone.

When the True Divine Light and Love live in someone, that person loves nothing else but God alone, because he or she loves God as Goodness and for the sake of Goodness, and all Goodness as One, and One as All. Because All is One and One is All in God.

CHAPTER 47

If We Are to Love All Things,
Must We Love Sin Too?

You may ask, "If we are to love all things, must we then love sin too?"

I answer, No, because when I say "all things," I mean all Good.

Everything is good because it is rooted in Being. Even the Devil is good because he has Being. In this sense (that is, in that the foundation of all things is Being and therefore good) nothing is evil or not good.

However, to sin is an act of will. It is to want otherwise than as God wills. This willing is not Being, and therefore it has no basis in the good. Things are only good in as much as they are in God and with God. Now all things have their Being in God, and more truly in God than in themselves, and therefore all things are good in as much as they have Being. If there were anything that did not have its Being in God, it would not be good. Willing or desiring that is contrary to God is not in God, because God cannot will or desire anything contrary to himself or otherwise than himself. Therefore, this willing is evil or not good and is even nothingness.

God also loves actions, but not all actions. Which ones then does he love? He loves those that are done from the instruction and guidance of the True Light and the True Love. Whatever is done from these, in these, and through these is done in spirit and in truth. These are God's, and they please him. However, what is done from the False Light and the False Love is all from the Devil. Especially whatever happens, is done, is left undone, is produced, or is suffered from any will other than God's will is from the Devil. These actions are without God and contrary to him. They are all completely contrary to good works and are, without exception, sinful.

CHAPTER 48

*We Must Believe in Spiritual Truth Before
We Can Understand or Experience It*

Christ said, "Whoever does not believe will be condemned" (Mark 16:16). This is true, for a person living in
this temporal world who has no understanding of spiritual things, will never get any without first believing.
Anyone who wants spiritual knowledge before believing
anything will never get any true knowledge.

We are not talking about the articles of the Christian
faith here, for they are known to everyone, whether sinful or saved, good or wicked. They must be believed in the
first place, because without believing them one cannot
come to know the very basics.

What we are talking about here is a certain type of
Truth, which is known through experiencing it. You have
to believe in it first before you can experience it, or else
you will never know it at all. This is the faith that Christ
spoke about in the saying above.

CHAPTER 49

*About Self-Will, and How Both Lucifer and
Adam Fell from Grace through Self-Will*

It has been said that there is more self-will in hell than
anything else. This is true, for there is nothing else in hell
apart from self-will, and if there were no self-will, there
would be no Devil and no hell.

When it is said that Lucifer fell from Heaven and
turned away from God, it means that he preferred his
own will and refused to conform to the Eternal Will. It
was the same thing with Adam in the Garden of Eden. In
simple terms, when we say self-will we mean to will
something other than as the one and Eternal Will of God
wills.

CHAPTER 50

This Temporal World Is a Paradise and an Outer Court of Heaven. There Is Only One Forbidden Fruit: Self-Will

What is Paradise? All things that exist, for everything is good and we can truly call this world a Paradise. It is also said that Paradise is an outer court of Heaven. This world is indeed an outer court of the Eternal or of Eternity. This is true because all things are rooted in the good, in Being, and they can be a guide and a path to God and Eternity. In this sense, this world is an outer court of Eternity, and it can well be called a Paradise, for it is one.

All things are allowed in this Paradise apart from one tree and its fruits. I mean that of all things that are, nothing is forbidden and nothing is contrary to God but one thing only. That is self-will, or to will otherwise than as the Eternal Will wills.

God said to Adam (and also to you and everyone), "Whatever you do or whatever happens, nothing is forbidden if it is not done from your will, but according to mine. Everything that you do from your own will is contrary to the Eternal Will."

Do not be paralyzed by thinking that everything that is done in this way is necessarily contrary to the Eternal Will. It is only in as far as it is done from a different will, or otherwise than from the Eternal or Divine Will.

CHAPTER 51

Why Did God Create Self-Will, Seeing That It Is So Contrary to Him?

You may ask, "Since this tree (that is, self-will) is so contrary to God and the Eternal Will, why did God create it and plant it in the Garden of Eden?"

I answer, People who want to understand the hidden mind and will of God, wanting to know why God does this or does not do that, desire the same thing as Adam and the Devil. This desire rarely comes from anything other than the delight in knowledge — it is all sheer pride. As long as this desire for intellectual glory lasts, the truth will never be known and people remain like Adam or the Devil.

A truly humble and enlightened person does not want God to reveal his secrets. This person does not ask why God does this or that, or stops this and allows that. Such a person wants only to know how to please God and to reduce the self to nothing, having no individual will so that the Eternal Will can live within, taking full possession of the self, unhindered by any other will. This person wants only to know how to best serve the Eternal Will.

However, this question can be answered in another way: The noblest gifts bestowed on any creature are reason and will. These two are so close that where you find one, the other is also there. Without them, there would be no reasoning creatures, but only unreasoning animals. This would be a great loss, because God would never be served or see himself and his attributes manifested in works, which they should be, as it is necessary for perfection.

Reason and knowledge are found together with will, with the intention that they can instruct the will and each other, so that neither reason nor will functions exclusively. Neither should dominate the other nor become dominant in its own right, because they belong to him from whom they proceed. They should submit to him, flow back into him, and become nothing, losing their identity and selfishness.

There is more about the will you need to know: There is an Eternal Will, which exists in God as a principle and a substance, but without any work or realization. This will is also in humanity or the creature, willing things, and then making them happen.

The primary quality of the will is that it should want to do something. What else is it for? It would exist for no purpose unless it had some work to do, and without the creature, it cannot achieve anything. Therefore, there must be creatures, and God has them so that the will can be exercised through them to achieve things that exist in

God, but are without realization. Therefore, the will in the creature, or the created will, is God's Eternal Will and does not belong to the creature. Because God cannot bring his will into existence without the creature, it pleases him to do it in and with the creature.

Therefore, the will is not meant to be exerted by the creature, but only by God, who has a right to work out his own will using the will which is in the creature but belongs to God. Where it is like this in anyone, God exerts the will, and not the person. Thus, it would not be self-will, because the person would not will anything other than as God wills. God himself would move the will and not the individual. The will would be one with the Eternal Will and flow into it, though the individual would still keep a sense of liking and disliking, pleasure and pain.

Wherever the will is exerted there must be a sense of liking and disliking, because when things go according to the individual's will a person likes it, and if they do not the person dislikes it. A person does not produce this liking and disliking but God does, because when the will comes from God and not from the individual, the liking and disliking come from him also.

There are no complaints apart from what is contrary to God, and there is no joy apart from him, that which is his, and that which belongs to him. It is the same with all the other powers of humans like perception, reason, gifts, and love. They are all from God, and not from humans. Where the will is completely surrendered to God, everything else is surrendered too. This is how God receives his due and how a person's will is not his or her own. God created the will for this and not for it to be self-will.

The Devil or Adam, or false nature, takes this will to itself, making it its own and using it for itself and its own purposes. This is the original sin, forbidden and contrary to God; it is the bite that Adam took from the apple.

If there is any self-will in a person, there can never be true peace or true rest. You can see this in both humans and the Devil. Neither can there ever be any holiness either in time or Eternity where this self-will is working; that is, where a person takes the will and makes it his or her own. If the will is not surrendered in the temporal world, but carried over into Eternity, it may never be surrendered. Then there is certainly no peace or holiness — just as we see in the Devil.

If there were no reason or will in the creatures, God would be unknown and unloved, and all the creatures would be worth nothing to God. Thus, I have answered the question of why God created the will.

When something is free, people cannot claim that it belongs to them. If they do, they are committing a wrong. Now, in the whole world nothing is as free as the will. When anybody tries to possess it and take it away from its excellent, unbounded freedom, that person is committing a wrong. This is what the Devil and Adam and all their followers do.

The right thing to do is to leave the will in its noble freedom, and this is what Christ and his followers do. If you rob the will of its noble freedom and own it for yourself, all you will get is care and trouble. Discontent, disquiet, unrest, and wretchedness will follow you both in this life and the next.

On the other hand, if you leave the will in its perfect freedom, you will have contentment, peace, rest, and holiness in this world and in Eternity. Where a person exists in whom the will is not enslaved, but continues noble and free, such a person is truly free, not a slave to anything. This is the one of whom Christ said, "The truth will set you free" and "If the Son sets you free, you will be free indeed" (John 8:32-36).

If you allow the will its freedom, you are using it correctly. If allowed to choose whatever it wants, it always chooses the noblest and the best, and it hates and is offended by all that is not noble and good. The more the will is free of self, the more it is offended by evil, injustice, and sin, and the more it is saddened by it. We can see this in Christ, whose will was the purest and the least fettered by self of any person who ever lived. Christ's human nature was also the freest of all creatures, and yet he felt deeper sadness and indignation at sin than any creature ever felt.

When people claim freedom for themselves and feel no sorrow or indignation at sin and what is contrary to God, when they say that we must pay attention to nothing and care about nothing, but be, in this present time, as Christ was after his resurrection, or as God is in his eternal aspect — this is not the true and divine freedom coming from the True Divine Light. Their freedom is a natural, false, satanic, and deceitful freedom, and it comes from a natural, false, and deluded light.

Were there is no self-will there is no ownership of the will and hence, no self-serving. The Kingdom of Heaven is like this, and there is peace and contentment. If anyone in the Kingdom of Heaven called anything his or her own, that individual would immediately be thrust out into hell and would become an evil spirit.

In hell, everybody has self-will and self-interest, and for that reason there is all manner of misery and wretchedness — just as there is here on earth. However, if one person in hell renounced self-will and called nothing his or her own, that individual would come straight out of hell into Heaven.

Now, in this world, a person is somewhere between Heaven and hell. A person can choose either. The more that this person has of ownership and self-will, the more he or she has of hell and misery. The less this person has of ownership and self-will, the less he or she has of hell, and the nearer this person is to the Kingdom of Heaven.

If a person can be completely free of self-will and ownership while still in this world, and be in God's True Light and abide in Being alone — this person would surely be in the Kingdom of Heaven.

If you have something, or seek or desire to have something of your own, you are owned as a slave. If you have nothing of your own, nor seek or desire anything for yourself, you are free and a slave to none.

Everything that has been said here, Christ taught in

words and in his life for thirty-three years. He taught it to us very briefly when he said, "Follow me" (Mark 8:34). But if you want to follow him, you must renounce everything, just as he renounced everything more completely than anyone else has ever done. If you want to come after him, you must take up the cross, and this cross is the Christ life, and it is a very bitter cross to nature. That is why he said, "Anyone who does not take his cross and follow me is not worthy of me [and] cannot be my disciple" (Matt. 10:38; Luke 14:27).

The natural person, in false freedom, believes that he or she has renounced everything. The truth is that this person wants nothing to do with the cross, saying "Enough of it already. I do not need it anymore." Such a person is deceived, and it is a shame, because if this person ever tasted the cross, he or she would never part with it. If you believe in Christ, you must believe everything that is written here.

CHAPTER 52

What Christ Meant by, "No One Comes
to the Father Except through Me"

Christ said, "No one comes to the Father except through me" (John 14:6). This is how to come to the Father through Christ: Watch over yourself, both inwardly and outwardly. Control and guard your heart as far as it is within your power. Do not allow any will, desire, opinion, or thought to spring up in it apart from those which are Godly or fitting for God, as if God lived in you. Whenever you become aware of any thought or intent rising up that does not belong to God or is not fitting for him, resist it and root it out thoroughly and quickly.

Order your outward behavior by this rule, whether at work or at leisure, in speech or in silence, sleeping or waking. In short: In every activity, in all of your dealings with yourself or others, keep your heart with all diligence. This is so that you can avoid doing anything or allowing anything to spring up in you that would not be fitting for God, or permissible if God lived in you.

If you stick to this, whatever you have in your innermost heart, and whatever your external actions, all will be of God, and you will be a follower of Christ in this life in the way I understand and write about.

If you lead a life like this, you can be said to "go in and out through Christ" and be a true follower of Christ. You will also go with Christ and through Christ to the Father.

You will also be a servant of Christ, for if you come after him you must be his servant, as he himself says: "Whoever serves me must follow me; and where I am, my servant also will be" (John 12:26).

If you are a servant and follower of Christ, you will come to that place where Christ himself is — that is, to the Father. As Christ says, "Father, I want those that you have given me to be with me where I am" (John 17:24). If you live your life in this way, you will "enter the sheep pen by the gate," that is, enter into eternal life, and "the watchman opens the gate for [you]" (John 10:1, 3).

Those who think they can enter by some other way or think that they can come to the Father or to eternal blessedness in a way other than through Christ are deceived, because they are not in the right Way and are not entering by the right Door. The watchman will not open the door to such a person for such a one is a thief and a murderer, as Christ says.

You cannot be in the right Way, or enter in by the right Door, if you are living in lawless freedom or in disregard of precepts of virtue and order. This behavior is not found in Christ, and neither is it in any of his true followers.

CHAPTER 53

What Christ Meant by, "No One Can Come to Me Unless the Father Who Sent Me Draws Him"

Christ said, "No one can come to me unless the Father who sent me draws him" (John 6:44). Now, I understand the Father to be the Perfect, Simple Good that is All and above All. Without it or beside it there is no True Substance or True Good, and no good work was ever or will be done without it.

As it is All, it must be in All and above All, hence it cannot be any of the things that the creatures, as creatures, can comprehend or understand. This is because whatever the creature, as a creature (that is, in its creaturely nature), can understand is something, this or that, and therefore is something like the creature itself. If the Simple, Perfect Good were something, this or that, that the creature could understand, it would not be the All or the Only One, and therefore it would not be Perfect. It also cannot be named because it is none of the things that the creature as creature can understand, know, or name.

When this Perfect Good, which is unnameable, flows

into a person and fills that person, we call it the Father because it brings out the Christ life in that person, and is itself in the Father.

When a part of this Perfect Good is granted to someone, as in a glance or a sudden revelation, the soul begins to long for the Perfect Good and to unite itself with the Father. As this yearning grows, more is revealed. The more that is revealed, the more it is drawn to the Father, and the more the yearning increases. In this way, the soul is drawn and increased in a union with the Eternal Goodness. This is the drawing of the Father, who instructs and draws a person to himself. One cannot enter into a union with him except through the Christ life. Such a person begins to put on that life of which I have spoken before.

I will now explain two sayings of Christ's:

The first one, "No one comes to the Father except through me" (John 14:6), means that a person comes to the Father through the Christ life, as I have said above.

The second one, "No one can come to me unless the Father who sent me draws him" (John 6:44), means that the Father grants a person a glimpse of the Perfect Good, and this draws that person to take on the Christ life.

This is the Perfect Good St. Paul is describing when he says, "when perfection comes, the imperfect disappears" (1 Cor. 13:10). That is, all created things are as nothing compared with the Perfect Good, because for the one who knows, feels, and tastes this Perfect Good, creatures become like nothing. Indeed, they are nothing, because without the Perfect One, there is neither True Good nor

Being. If you have, know, or love the Perfect One, you have and know all Goodness. What more can you want, either in your own self or in others, when everything is one Perfect Good?

I have here been referring to the outward life, but this life is only an access or portal to the inward life; the true inward life begins after this.

When one has tasted the Perfect, in as far as a person is able to do so in this world, all created things and even the self become nothing. Once such a person has seen the truth that the Perfect One is All and above All, that person must follow it. That person sees that all that is good, such as Being, Life, Knowledge, Reason, and Power, resides in the One and not in any creature. It follows then that this person does not claim to possess Being, Life, Knowledge, Reason and Power, Doing or Refraining, or anything that we can call good. In this way, a person becomes so empty as to be nothing, and such a person feels the same way about all things that mean something, that is, all created things.

A true inward life then begins in this person, because God himself lives in this person, and nothing is left but what is God's or of God, and nothing is left which takes anything for itself. And thus God himself, that is, the one Eternal Perfectness alone, is, lives, knows, works, loves, wills, does, and refrains in the person. This is how it should be; where it is not so, a person still has a long way to go and things are not completely right.

Another good way into this life is always to think that

what is best is the dearest, always to prefer the best, always to cling to it and unite oneself to it. In the creatures, the best is where the Eternal Perfect Goodness most brightly shines and works, and where it is best known and loved. This is what is of God and belongs to him. It is whatever we do with justice and truth, or what we might call good.

When someone holds on to that which is the best that can be discerned in the creatures, keeping to it alone with singleness of purpose, that person will come to what is better and better, until at last finding and tasting that the Eternal Good is Perfect Good, without measure, and above all created good.

If we love what is best, we follow its calling on our lives, and we love the one Eternal Good above all. We must cling to it alone and unite ourselves with it as closely as we can.

If we believe all Goodness comes from, and belongs to, the one Eternal Good (which is the truth, and therefore the right thing to believe) we should also attribute to him the beginning, middle, and end of our ways, so that nothing remains either to the individual person or to the creature (which is also the right thing to do). This is how it should be, whatever anybody says.

In this way, we arrive at the true inward life. What happens after this to the soul, or is revealed to it, no one can say or guess. This inner life has never been spoken of nor can it ever be fully understood by anyone.

I have told you what is right and what is true, that is,

that a person should claim nothing for self, nor should this person be moved to desire, will, love, or intend anything but by God alone or the one, Eternal, Perfect Goodness.

You will over-reach yourself and cause a rift with God if you claim anything for yourself, this or that, whatever it might be, contrary to the Eternal and Perfect Goodness that is God himself. It will keep you back from the perfect life.

You cannot reach the Perfect Good unless you forsake all things and principally your own self. Nobody can serve two masters who are contrary to one another. You must choose one and let the other go. Be assured of this: If the Creator is to enter in, the creature must depart.

CHAPTER 54

Do Not Seek Your Own Good Either in Spiritual or Natural Things, But Seek the Honor of God Alone, and Enter into Eternal Life by the Right Door, Which Is Christ

Become to God what your right hand is to you. If it is given to you to get this far, be content and seek nothing further. This is my spiritual direction, and I take my stand upon it: You must struggle with all your strength to be obedient to God so thoroughly, at all times, and in all things, that there is nothing left in you that opposes God. Then your soul and body stand ready and willing to do what God has created them for. As ready and willing as your right hand is, being so wholly in your power that in the twinkling of an eye you move and turn it wherever you want.

If it is not like this, then we must do our best to become like it, doing it from love and not fear, and in everything seek the glory and praise of God alone. We must not seek our own good, either in spiritual or natural things. It cannot be any other way for us. (In fact, every creature owes this to God by right, especially humans, who should be subject to God alone, God having given us stewardship over all creatures.)

Watch out if you have come so far, that you do not think you have achieved it yourself. The Devil is waiting to put his evil seed in your heart so that your natural self will take all the credit. You will then fall into foolish lawlessness and licentiousness, which is completely alien to and opposed to the true life in God.

This happens to the person who has not entered, or refuses to enter, by the right Way and the right Door (which is Christ, as we have said). This person imagines that he or she can arrive at the highest truth by another way or can even believe that he or she has already arrived, but such a person is certainly mistaken.

Christ is our witness, who says, "I tell you the truth, the man who does not enter the sheep pen by the gate, but climbs in by some other way, is a thief and a robber" (John 10:1). This person is a thief because he or she robs God of his honor and glory. They belong to God alone, but the thief takes them for the self. This person is a murderer because he or she kills his or her own soul, taking away its life, which is God. Just as the body lives by the soul, so the soul lives by God.

This person also murders all who follow his or her teaching and example. Christ said, "I have come down from heaven not to do my own will but to do the will of him who sent me" (John 6:38). And "Why do you call me, 'Lord, Lord'?" (Luke 6:46), as if to say, it will not help you to eternal life.

And again Christ said, "Not everyone who says to me, 'Lord, Lord,' will enter into the kingdom of heaven, but only he who does the will of my Father who is in heaven" (Matt. 7:21). Christ also said, "If you want to enter life, obey the commandments" (Matt. 19:17). And what are the commandments? "Love the Lord your God with all your heart and with all your soul and with all your strength and with all your mind; and love your neighbor as yourself" (Luke 10:27). These two commandments sum up all the others.

There is nothing more precious to God or more profitable for a person than humble obedience. In God's eyes, one good work done from true obedience is of more value than a hundred thousand done from self-will, contrary to obedience. Therefore, whoever has this obedience does not need to fear God's disapproval, for this person is in the right way and following Christ.

May we deny ourselves, renouncing and forsaking all things for God.

May we give up our own wills, living for God alone and to his holy will.

May he help us, who gave up his will to his Heavenly Father — our Lord Jesus Christ, upon whom be blessings forever and ever.

Amen.